Samuel French Acting Edition

The Plot

by Will Eno

∥SAMUEL FRENCH∥

Copyright © 2020 by Will Eno
All Rights Reserved

THE PLOT is fully protected under the copyright laws of the United States of America, the British Commonwealth, including Canada, and all member countries of the Berne Convention for the Protection of Literary and Artistic Works, the Universal Copyright Convention, and/or the World Trade Organization conforming to the Agreement on Trade Related Aspects of Intellectual Property Rights. All rights, including professional and amateur stage productions, recitation, lecturing, public reading, motion picture, radio broadcasting, television and the rights of translation into foreign languages are strictly reserved.

ISBN 978-0-573-70881-7

www.concordtheatricals.com
www.concordtheatricals.co.uk

FOR PRODUCTION ENQUIRIES

UNITED STATES AND CANADA
info@concordtheatricals.com
1-866-979-0447

UNITED KINGDOM AND EUROPE
licensing@concordtheatricals.co.uk
020-7054-7200

Each title is subject to availability from Concord Theatricals Corp., depending upon country of performance. Please be aware that *THE PLOT* may not be licensed by Concord Theatricals Corp. in your territory. Professional and amateur producers should contact the nearest Concord Theatricals Corp. office or licensing partner to verify availability.

CAUTION: Professional and amateur producers are hereby warned that *THE PLOT* is subject to a licensing fee. The purchase, renting, lending or use of this book does not constitute a license to perform this title(s), which license must be obtained from Concord Theatricals Corp. prior to any performance. Performance of this title(s) without a license is a violation of federal law and may subject the producer and/or presenter or such performances to civil penalties. A licensing fee must be paid whether the title(s) is presented for charity or gain and whether or not admission is charged. Professional/Stock licensing fees are quoted upon application to Concord Theatricals Corp.

This work is published by Samuel French, an imprint of Concord Theatricals Corp.

No one shall make any changes in this title(s) for the purpose of production. No part of this book may be reproduced, stored in a retrieval system, or transmitted in any form, by any means, now known or yet to be invented, including mechanical, electronic, photocopying, recording, videotaping, or otherwise, without the prior written permission of the publisher. No one shall upload this title(s), or part of this title(s), to any social media websites.

For all enquiries regarding motion picture, television, and other media rights, please contact Concord Theatricals Corp.

MUSIC USE NOTE

Licensees are solely responsible for obtaining formal written permission from copyright owners to use copyrighted music in the performance of this play and are strongly cautioned to do so. If no such permission is obtained by the licensee, then the licensee must use only original music that the licensee owns and controls. Licensees are solely responsible and liable for all music clearances and shall indemnify the copyright owners of the play(s) and their licensing agent, Concord Theatricals Corp., against any costs, expenses, losses and liabilities arising from the use of music by licensees. Please contact the appropriate music licensing authority in your territory for the rights to any incidental music.

IMPORTANT BILLING AND CREDIT REQUIREMENTS

If you have obtained performance rights to this title, please refer to your licensing agreement for important billing and credit requirements.

THE PLOT's world premiere was produced by Yale Repertory Theatre in New Haven, Connecticut (James Bundy, Artistic Director; Victoria Nolan, Managing Director) and premiered on December 2, 2019. The performance was directed by Oliver Butler, with scenic design by Sarah Karl, costume design by April M. Hickman, lighting design by Evan C. Anderson, and sound design and original music by Emily Duncan Wilson. The stage manager was Fabiola Syvel. The cast was as follows:

JOANNE .... Mia Katigbak
RIGHTY .... Harris Yulin
TIM .... Stephen Barker Turner
DONNA .... Jennifer Mudge
GREY .... Jimonn Cole

THE PLOT was commissioned by Steppenwolf Theatre Company in Chicago, Illinois (Martha Lavey, Artistic Director; David Hawkanson, Executive Director).

CHARACTERS

Casting should be inclusive, with a cast that reflects the contemporary world. For all characters, a natural, unpretentious kind of acting that is specific, deep, but also easeful is best. The play should move fairly briskly.

JOANNE – Sixties/seventies, capable, grounded, a little beleaguered with her life and her caretaking duties, she has a private, dry sense of humor.

RIGHTY – Sixties/seventies, seems to be struggling with mental issues but never descends into full-on confusion. There is a sharpness to him that many dementia and Alzheimer's patients can display, where on certain topics they are comfortable and confident. He probably wears a similar outfit most of the time, and maybe it's a little preppy, although it seems Joanne dresses him. A New England type.

TIM – Forties/fifties, a real estate developer, he thinks and speaks quickly. He believes that his insults and criticisms are good advice so he dispenses these in a way that almost sounds gentle and reasonable. He also doesn't linger too much with an insult – he just lightly moves on, which is probably worse. He is fairly successful at what he does, though he has not yet had a huge triumph, and his financial situation is somewhat precarious.

DONNA – Thirties/forties, professional and smart, she has committed to the real estate industry. She is making a push to really get her life together and is almost there.

GREY – Thirties/forties, male, Black, he's fairly private, fairly self-reliant. He's both a Science and Math type, and also an Arts and Nature type, but he doesn't need people to know these things about himself. He has an idea of where he wants to go in life but isn't fully there yet.

SETTING

A small country graveyard.

AUTHOR'S NOTES

Downstage, at stage right, are two angled, moss-covered, and worn gravestones. Near them is one small, new gravestone. Off to the back is a rectangular hole in the ground, marked off with faded yellow tape, where a grave, many months ago, has been disinterred. Upstage right, extending halfway across the stage, is a brick wall covered with vines, moss, and lichen. This is the long side of an old building that was used for equipment and materials storage in busier days. A pathway winds past the side of the building, back toward a parking lot. A sign that says, "Briarwood Cemetery." Stage left, and up a small rise, is an old gazebo, painted white but peeling (with a missing section of roof, if necessary for sight lines). Stage right is the gravestone area, and slightly elevated, at stage left, is the gazebo area. Trees and a stone wall, to the back and side, if space allows. Off to the side, almost invisible in weeds and brush, some statuary, including a small, broken angel statue.

Transitions should be done as speedily and cleanly as possible, accompanied by sounds (and perhaps subtle projections) of the natural world.

A sound note: There are occasional text messages and emails which arrive on people's phones that are instrumental to the play. In addition, a production should add some additional text alert sounds (seven or so) throughout the play, that people quickly look at and then ignore, or delete, as in life. This is so that not every single message that arrives is of serious consequence.

Deep bow to enthusiasm, deep bow to Martha Lavey.

Scene One

Nighttime in a small, country graveyard.

JOANNE *enters with a strong flashlight, moving carefully in the dark. Sounds of a distant freight train. Some frogs and crickets and nighttime sounds.*

JOANNE. Righty? Are you out here? *(Brief pause.)* Righty? *(To herself:)* I hate this place. *(Very brief pause.)* Are you here?

RIGHTY *sits up from where he's been hiding, somewhere behind* **JOANNE** *and off to the side.*

RIGHTY. Yup. Here I am.

JOANNE. *(Startled:)* Oh God. Why didn't you answer?

RIGHTY. I didn't hear you.

JOANNE. Well, obviously, you did.

RIGHTY. Oh, you're right – that's true.

Some lights come up as **JOANNE** *sweeps her flashlight around, but it remains a shadowy scene.*

JOANNE. You can't keep wandering off. You didn't hear your phone?

RIGHTY. It's for emergencies.

JOANNE. And how did you know this wasn't one?

RIGHTY. You got me again.

JOANNE. You're driving me crazy.

RIGHTY. I don't keep wandering off. I go for walks.

He stands and brushes himself off, but remains to the side.

JOANNE. I spent an hour looking for you over on the Cabot Pasture. You said, "I'm going over to the Cabot Pasture."

RIGHTY. But I wasn't. I was here.

JOANNE. I see that.

RIGHTY. I don't go a lot of places. I'm either here or there.

JOANNE. *(Looks around.)* It's morbid.

RIGHTY. I like it.

JOANNE. I know, I know – you like how the moss feels. You feel it growing around you when you lie down. But it's morbid. Maybe it's nice for a zombie.

RIGHTY. *(Very slight effort at an impersonation:)* I'm not a zombie – I'm an Elephant Man.

JOANNE. Someone's been staying up watching movies.

RIGHTY. *I* have. Who told you that?

JOANNE. Let's get you home.

RIGHTY. Okay. Don't worry.

JOANNE. Says the man who puts his socks in the refrigerator.

RIGHTY. The TV said it helps the cholesterol.

JOANNE. Well, it doesn't, and I doubt the TV said that. This is why I don't let you answer the phone at home anymore. Remember, you almost bought a trailer for a boat?

RIGHTY. Yup. *(Small self-deprecating laugh.)* You put a stop to that.

JOANNE. Doesn't even own a boat and the man is halfway through his credit card number to buy a trailer for it. Over the phone, from a stranger in a different state.

RIGHTY. Oops. But this is different.

JOANNE. What is? Come on, silly old man, let's go.

> **RIGHTY** *sits on the new gravestone.*

No, don't sit down – we're going. Besides, it's disrespectful.

RIGHTY. This is my place. Just give me a minute.

JOANNE. Get off of that. How would you like it if you were Mr. or Mrs. –

She tries to read the gravestone, but **RIGHTY**'s *legs are in the way.*

RIGHTY. I wouldn't mind.

JOANNE. Well, that's fine, but you're not Mr. – *(She's able to read.)* Oh my God. What is this?

RIGHTY. *(Stands.)* My name.

JOANNE. I see that.

RIGHTY. *(Admiring the gravestone:)* Richard "Righty" Morse. It's official.

JOANNE. What's official? When did you do this?

RIGHTY. A little while ago. *(Admires the gravestone.)* I got a ninety-nine-year lease. I guess that's how long eternity is, these days.

JOANNE. No. We took care of all this, remember? We got the deal at Greenview Memorial through your union. We're side by side, under a willow tree.

RIGHTY. We were only looking at that.

JOANNE. No. We put a deposit. A non-refundable deposit.

RIGHTY. I want to be here.

JOANNE. How much did this cost?

RIGHTY. They said it was a good investment.

JOANNE. Oh, I'm sure they did, but here's what they didn't tell you: it isn't. At all. I can see the pamphlet: "This is a good investment. Asterisk, footnote: This is a terrible investment." I can't even…this was the big shrewd move you were bragging about, your safety net – a hole in the ground for when you're dead?

RIGHTY. Well, when you say it like –

JOANNE. – That's how you say it. That's what the words are that describe this. *(Brief pause.)* How much?

RIGHTY. It's from the savings.

JOANNE. How much?

RIGHTY. I said, the savings.

JOANNE. Oh God. We have to go. We have to fix this. I don't even know who to talk to. And I just have to ask, where did your plan leave me?

RIGHTY. You don't like it here.

JOANNE. No, I don't. *(Brief pause.)* Do you ever think about anyone other than yourself? Even just by accident? *(Very brief pause.)* You know, it hurts, it's really hurtful. Every minute of the day, I'm thinking about you, whether I want to or not.

RIGHTY. No. Joanne. *(Points to the area next to his gravestone.)* This is yours.

JOANNE. Without a gravestone.

RIGHTY. I thought you'd want to choose your own.

JOANNE. And not be on one together with you?

RIGHTY. And have to see your name right there, when you visit every week?

JOANNE. Every week? What, are you going to open up a dry cleaner's here, too?

RIGHTY. I thought you'd want to put a poem on it or a song and I wanted you to have room. Space.

JOANNE. Yes, I probably would.

RIGHTY. Let's get me home.

JOANNE. *(Noticing something:)* What was that? Something just moved.

She searches with the flashlight.

RIGHTY. *(Looks around, then sees it, looks closer.)* Salamander.

JOANNE. *(Noticing something else on the ground:)* Is that bottle yours?

RIGHTY. Yeah. *(Picks up a half-filled plastic water bottle.)* I know I can't get around like I used to.

JOANNE. It's not that, Righty. It's, you forget everything. It's your mind.

RIGHTY. It's my mind. *(Gestures to gravestone.)* This makes me calm. I'm not crazy.

JOANNE. Nobody said you were crazy.

RIGHTY. *(Brief pause.)* Listen to how quiet it is. I mean, *(Points at his mouth.)* except... *(Quietly:)* So quiet – except for me talking right now.

JOANNE. It is quiet. *(Very brief pause. Gently:)* Ooh, you know what I think I just heard starting up? The sound of *me* talking right now. *(Regular voice, but somewhat relentless:)* Do you know what my medicine costs? Or your constant care, when I can't do it anymore? Or what every little day of our very little future is going to cost? Do you have any idea what any of this is like for me? That's the worst part.

> *Brief pause.* **RIGHTY**'s *moved into some darkness and turned away.*

(To herself:) It's like talking to a brick wall.

RIGHTY. No, it isn't.

JOANNE. A selfish, financially irresponsible brick wall.

RIGHTY. I just want somewhere, Jo. One place, that stays. So everybody doesn't forget.

JOANNE. I'm not going to forget you, Righty.

RIGHTY. You're old. You'll be gone soon, too.

JOANNE. *(Quietly:)* Yes, thank you. My husband, the bucket of cold water.

RIGHTY. I'm sorry for whatever I did. I know I can't get around like I used to.

> *He moves into the light. There's a large, wet stain on the crotch of his trousers.*

JOANNE. "Whatever you did"? What you did was throw away our entire – oh, God. Did you have an accident?

RIGHTY. *(Looking down:)* Well, I didn't do it on purpose.

JOANNE. Well, okay, let's get you home, you need to change. Can you see all right?

RIGHTY. Not too good. Certain things.

> *Lights. They exit.*

Scene Two

Morning in the graveyard. Slanting sunlight and some birdsong. **TIM**, *a real estate developer, is there with* **DONNA**, *his assistant. Both are wearing comfortable business attire.*

TIM. Your photos don't do it justice.

DONNA. It was cloudy.

TIM. Cloudy is good for photographs. Don't blame the actual world for your crappy picture of it.

DONNA. I just mean, it was hard to get the, like, the exact right –

TIM. *(Interrupting:)* – Life's tough.

> **GREY**, *dressed in professional/outdoorsy clothes, appears by the gazebo, stops to take a note. He's carrying a sketchpad and a messenger bag.*

(Quietly:) Who's this guy, again?

DONNA. *(Quietly:)* Historical commission, I think?

TIM. Yuck.

DONNA. I think they're concerned that some of the older –

GREY. – What's that? *(Comes closer.)* Such a beautiful spot, huh?

TIM. Totally. It's got that special "je ne sais feng shui."

GREY. I don't know that exact phrase, but, yes.

TIM. You're with the H-Comm right?

GREY. No. The what? Oh, the Historical Commission. Yeah, but nobody says it like that.

TIM. Thought I'd take a stab. I'm Tim Tyson.

GREY. Hi. Grey. Grey Little.

A small smile from **DONNA**.

TIM. What's that look? You have a secret to divulge?

DONNA. No. Hi. I've heard your name. Grey Little sounds like a character in a children's book.

GREY. Um, nope. I'm a grown-up in the actual world.

DONNA. No, it's nice. Hi. I'm Donna Sones.

GREY. Hi. I have no comment about your name.

TIM. My brother-in-law's name is also Greg. Not my favorite person in the world, but, you're probably okay. *(Very brief pause.)* That's 100-year-old moss, right there.

GREY. At least. It's actually Grey, my name. Like the color. I'll be overseeing the disinterments, should there be any more. It's important to us that as much as possible of the history here is preserved in any final development plans.

TIM. Great. We'll figure all that out. It's from needing nitrogen, the moss. The earth is sour, it needs nitrogen.

GREY. That's right. You treat it with lime. I'm also a landscape architect.

TIM. Great. *(A very brief pause.)*

TIM.	**GREY.**
So, we should probably...	I really love...

GREY. Go ahead.

TIM. No, please – what were you saying?

GREY. Just, I love when nature and humans make something beautiful together, that neither could've made on their own. The moss on a grave, the dandelion coming through the sidewalk. It's just, I don't know, it's special.

TIM. Huh. I thought you were going to say something better than that.

GREY. Um, nope. I guess it was just that.

DONNA. *(To **TIM**:)* So, nitrogen, huh? I'm impressed. You're quite the expert.

TIM. I mowed lawns when I was a kid.

DONNA. Still, I'm impressed.

TIM. I'm your boss and mentor. Et cetera. What else are you going to be? Sad? Hugely disappointed? Enraged? *(To **GREY**, with some amusement:)* Right? Fucking enraged that her boss once did landscaping? I don't think so. Wouldn't make any sense.

DONNA. No, come on. I'm saying it's great you know about different things.

TIM. Fine. Moving on. *(As he looks around:)* This really is a great spot. Lot of potential.

DONNA. You've been talking about developing this for a while.

TIM. And now we will. First order of business, though, is cleaning it all up. Paul Neubatten – you know that name, right?

DONNA. Yeah, he did Market Square, and the Brentmoor.

GREY. I worked on the Brentmoor.

DONNA. You did?

GREY. He gets terrible migraines. I never actually met him.

TIM. Neubatten's agreed to bankroll the whole thing. Once we muddle through all the red tape and dead bodies. No one wants to get involved in a rat's nest.

DONNA. That's really incredible. Congratulations.

TIM. And to you, too. Because you're going to be my right-hand woman.

DONNA. Tim. Wow. This is amazing. When you said you had news, I thought it was something else.

TIM. You sound disappointed.

DONNA. No, my God, are you kidding? This is incredible.

GREY. Well, there's a couple big question marks, here.

TIM. There's a couple big question marks everywhere.

*He looks at **GREY** and yawns.*

Man, I was up so late. I think I drank too much. Too much alcohol for my organs to, you know, handle. Metabolize. *(Remembering that **DONNA** and he were together:)* Oh, that's right, you were there.

DONNA. I'd never been to that place, Cardigan's.

TIM. I used to bartend there, back in the day. *(Shaking off another yawn:)* Whoo.

***GREY** moves off to make some notes.*

DONNA. *(Quietly:)* I cannot get over this, Tim. So amazing. Hey, are we still on for dinner tonight?

TIM. We are not, sadly. Sorry. *(Looking at gravestones:)* I know our relationship is a little muddy.

DONNA. It is, isn't it. But it feels good just to acknowledge it. *(Very brief pause.)* Were you going to say something else?

TIM. No, that was the full remark. "Our relationship is a little muddy." Did you start looking into any of this stuff, moving the graves?

DONNA. *(Looking into a folder:)* Yeah, I'm on it. *(Referring to the hole with the faded yellow tape around it:)* This one's already been moved.

TIM. Yeah? The empty hole in the ground? That one's already been moved? Thank you.

DONNA. Yes, obviously – sorry.

TIM. No, no apology necessary. You explained something that was fairly self-explanatory. It's not a tragedy. We just move on. Wasn't there a historical one?

DONNA. It was in the back, there. I think it was a relative of one of the presidents.

GREY. Yes, a cousin of Franklin Pierce. The town took care of that.

TIM. Good. *(Looks around.)* If I was the type to sigh, I'd probably sigh right now.

DONNA. And why is that?

TIM. I really don't like that phrase. "And why is that."

DONNA. No, I know. I was just...

TIM. *(Brief pause.)* Dot dot dot. People who trail off don't do well in the business arena. You can't trail off.

DONNA. Of course. So, I'm arranging a meeting –

TIM. *(Interrupting, with a small gesture and sounds:)* Uhp, uhp, uhp. And here comes a forceful and declarative statement. Noted. *(Very brief pause.)* Anywho...actually, that's exactly it: "Anywho." A person is born, it's some president's cousin, a future math whiz, or a skinny little baby with terrible allergies. Our little Anywho lives and grows, learns to talk and gets a job, has affairs and kids and setbacks, changes of heart, deathbed conversions, and then, the dust becomes dust. And Little Anywho is laid to his or her eternal rest, until someone comes along, me in this case, and says, "Hey, you know what, let's move this shit and put something else here."

DONNA. Well, it's progress. Time marches –

TIM. *(Interrupts, as if saying, "Don't interrupt, I'm on a roll":)* – I'm developing a little thing, here. *(Back to his thing:)* "I had a bad dream. I don't want to go to school today. I don't know if Houston is really the city for me." All the questions and doubts, the maps and college brochures, all to end up here. And then from here to wherever some incredibly handsome and shrewd businessman says you should go. *(Very brief pause.)* I had an uncle who wanted to be buried in blue jeans with his Swiss Army knife. I was too young to understand. *(Very brief pause.)* I still totally don't, to be honest.

DONNA. This is a very poetic side of you.

TIM. Normally, I swear more, but, you know… *(Gestures, as if to say, "Look where we are.")* My mom wrote poetry. She was cremated. Her ashes are…where are they? *(Thinks, remembers.)* Wow, this is shitty – I think they're in storage.

DONNA. I'm sorry.

TIM. So am I. If I want to visit with my mom, I've got to fight through a pile of beanbag chairs and downhill skis.

Distant sound of a train whistle.

DONNA. You're not having second thoughts?

TIM. Please. I barely have first thoughts.

DONNA. So we're going ahead?

TIM. Where else would we go? *(Quietly:)* Where else? Moss always makes me sentimental.

DONNA. I know what you mean.

TIM. *(Instantly, a challenge:)* And what do I mean?

DONNA. No, I'm saying, I could totally understand –

TIM. *(Interrupting:)* I'll interrupt you before you fail to finish that sentence. Let some things lie, okay. *(Little laugh as he points at the gravestones.)* But not these things. *(To* **GREY***:)* Right, Greg? Dig these fucking things up and get rid of them. Oops. Swear word in a graveyard, minus ten points.

GREY. It's Grey.

TIM. Coulda used those ten points, too.

DONNA. So, it's just those two old ones, over there. And the new one.

GREY. *(Looking at the new gravestone.)* He hasn't even died, yet. It just has the date of birth. Richard "Righty" Morse.

TIM. Well, well. Lucky Richard Righty Morse. What is that – the guy has a nickname for being right-handed? It's like my buddy, "Two Eyes" McGinley. *(To* **DONNA***, gesturing to Righty's grave:)* Where are we with him?

DONNA. I've tried to make contact.

TIM. Wow, you're amazing, thank you so much.

DONNA. No, I mean, I will. I've had trouble reaching –

TIM. – At least there's only a few left.

DONNA. Nobody wants to get buried here, since the new cemetery got built. Still, the last few plots were pretty expensive. I get the feeling Mr. Morse and his wife don't have a lot of money, so I guess it was important to them.

TIM. Find him and take care of him, all right?

DONNA. And, by "take care of him," I'm supposed to –

TIM. – Jesus. I'm not talking Mafia code. Go speak with Mr. Morse or his family and find an acceptable alternative.

DONNA. So, I'll offer them replacement cost, plus –

TIM. – Offer whatever. Offer a rose garden. We need to level this place in three weeks. Otherwise, Neubatten backs out and the whole thing goes "kaboom," except quieter than that. And I'm in on this thing with my own money. I need this.

A quick kiss or intimate gesture with **DONNA**.

Big life changes coming up.

DONNA. Yes. It's all going to happen.

TIM. If this goes good, we're in line for Neubatten's other projects and he's doing some really big stuff. That's why I don't mind taking on some debt to get this done.

DONNA. You're going to see a side of me you don't know yet.

TIM. Great, can't wait. And can you make a reservation at the Garrison for two, tonight. It's me and the wife. Put it in Victoria's name – they always give her a better table. *(He acknowledges the ugliness of the request:)* I know, I know. Patience. The world is the world.

DONNA. Okay. But, sometimes, this is really hard for me.

TIM. I know. But, just remember…yeah, the world is the world. I was going to say something different but actually I think that was pretty good. Ciao. *(Exits.)*

DONNA. Okay, bye. *(As she's making a note:)* I'm going to make sure that all this…

TIM *is gone.*

(Sadly:) Dot dot dot.

Brief pause. A chickadee sings.

GREY. Chickadee.

DONNA *looks at* **GREY**.

That's what kind of bird. "My little chickadee."

DONNA. You look like you're expecting me to say something back.

Lights change. Nighttime sounds. A shooting star low in the trees or some other distant natural event.

Scene Three

Late morning in the graveyard, a few days later.

JOANNE *and* **RIGHTY** *are standing near the gazebo.* **JOANNE** *has a thermos of tea. A few moments pass.*

RIGHTY. We're just standing here?

JOANNE. We're waiting for the young woman to come back. She said she forgot something.

RIGHTY. What'd she forget? I don't think she's coming back.

JOANNE. I'm sure she's coming back.

RIGHTY. I'm going to use the men's room.

He heads off, passing **DONNA** *just as she appears.*

DONNA. Don't you want to join us, while we figure this out?

RIGHTY. Hi.

He exits.

DONNA *is holding a package of biscuits and some paperwork.*

DONNA. Shall we sit? *(Gestures toward the gazebo.)*

They sit. **DONNA** *sets the biscuits down and offers them to* **JOANNE**.

Please. I forgot I'd gotten these. In case you didn't have breakfast.

JOANNE. No, thank you. I'd prefer we just begin.

DONNA. Okay. I had this contract drawn up and I just need your signature and then we're done. *(She pulls out a simple one-page contract.)* We void the lease on the plot here, and you get your money back.

JOANNE. I just want Righty to know I'm on his side. And I am on his side. *(Brief pause.)* Which, to be honest with you, it can be a very lonely place.

DONNA. *(She can imagine it.)* I can't imagine.

JOANNE. I don't know if you know anything about Alzheimer's? He seems like the old Righty when he talks about the graveyard here. I tell him it's morbid.

DONNA. Well, I guess the idea of it must give him some peace.

JOANNE. Maybe, but why doesn't he… I'm sure you're right, it probably gives him some peace. *(Looking at the contract:)* It's just one piece of paper?

DONNA. Yes. Very simple.

JOANNE. And that's for both?

DONNA. What? You'd both need to sign, yes.

JOANNE. That doesn't help us with the money we lost at the first cemetery, the deposit. It doesn't even get us back to zero. *(Slumps a little.)* Maybe I should just leave it like it is, so at least Righty's happy.

RIGHTY. *(From offstage:)* Joanne! Jo!

JOANNE. *(Loudly:)* I'm right here! We're in the gazebo!

RIGHTY. *(Brief pause. From offstage:)* The what?! I'm okay.

JOANNE. He doesn't recognize things and gets scared.

DONNA. Oh, wow.

JOANNE. Sometimes it's a mirror.

DONNA. Oh, the poor man. And you.

JOANNE. You should see us in that dank little apartment, two ghosts bumping around, afraid of everything. What is your Mr. Tyson building again? Luxury condos?

DONNA. It's a transfer station. Rail-to-truck shipping and distribution. They did a geologic survey, and this was the best spot. Plus, because of where the train line is.

JOANNE. *(With a kind of "case closed" feel:)* Well, but this is where we're supposed to be buried.

DONNA. I hope we can find some other options. I drew up a few different alternatives. *(Takes a five-page contract out of her bag.)* This'll provide for that same voiding of the lease, in addition to a cash payment, above and beyond the deposit you lost at the other cemetery. I just want you to feel taken care of.

JOANNE. I guess Righty did too. With the plot next to him.

DONNA. With the...sorry?

> *She checks through her paperwork to see if there's a record of another plot.*

JOANNE. *(Referring to the biscuits:)* I changed my mind. May I?

DONNA. Please.

> **JOANNE** *gets a biscuit and takes a bite.*

JOANNE. There's a certain logic to that man. Not logic, but something. *(Very brief pause.)* Can you believe, I thought we'd travel. I spent thirty-one years going to the same office.

DONNA. *(Very brief pause.)* Wow.

JOANNE. Would you like to know what I did?

DONNA. I didn't want to interrupt.

JOANNE. I had stopped talking.

DONNA. No, of course. What did you do?

JOANNE. It's not important. Does it ever occur to you that an older person might just like to be heard?

DONNA. Of course, I'm sorry if I've –

JOANNE. – Not answered back to, but, heard. Particularly given my husband's condition?

DONNA. I – yes. I'm sorry.

JOANNE. A home aide comes over a couple days a week. She's nice but it's not like having a friend listen.

DONNA. And I'm sure it's expensive.

JOANNE. We get some help. Anyway, I thought we'd travel. I even had a silly dream we could sail. Righty grew up around boats. *(Very brief pause.)* I was a secretary for a tomato wholesaler.

DONNA. Oh, wow. Tomatoes. That must've been really...

JOANNE. *(After waiting for **DONNA** to complete the sentence:)* Yeah, there really are no words to describe it. Righty worked at a ceramic tile factory. We toiled away and collected travel brochures.

DONNA. I do that.

JOANNE. I used to be a more interesting person. I was depressed, even suicidal, but then Righty got sick and I thought, "What's the point?"

DONNA. Is that – are you serious?

JOANNE. What do you think?

DONNA. Oh, Joanne.

JOANNE. Thank you.

DONNA. Maybe we could get back to what I'm proposing?

JOANNE. You're very persistent.

DONNA. Well, it's an exciting moment.

JOANNE. *(Brief pause.)* I really don't know what you want me to do.

DONNA. Well... I want you to look at this little piece of land with me, and see if we can imagine it in some different way.

JOANNE. *(Gets up with some difficulty and exits.)* My glasses are in the car.

> *(**DONNA** cross-checks some documents, her phone, etc. **RIGHTY** quietly appears, in an accidentally startling way.)*

DONNA. Oh, hello! Wow. You're very quiet.

RIGHTY. Where is she?

DONNA. She went to the car.

RIGHTY. Are you the one that wants to give us the house?

DONNA. What? Sorry, that's in exchange for your place there?

RIGHTY. *(Looks at her closely for a moment.)* It was someone else. It was a man with white hair.

DONNA. People are really interested, huh?

RIGHTY. I just want a good afterlife. And the one before that. *(Brief pause.)* Don't look at me like that. I know I get... *(Makes a "confused" gesture, twirling a finger around the side of his head.)* but, just take care of us, because I know what is what.

DONNA. I know you do. And, what is it?

RIGHTY. What?

DONNA. What is what?

RIGHTY. Ha ha. Very funny. *(Very brief pause.)* Were you trying to be funny?

DONNA. I wasn't.

RIGHTY. Well, I'm not surprised.

JOANNE. *(From offstage:)* Richard? Righty?

RIGHTY. *(Quietly:)* I need to use the facilities again. I have to go all the time. I'm like a, *(Searches briefly for a metaphor.)* I don't know, something that urinates a lot.

> *He exits.*
>
> **JOANNE** *enters with reading glasses.*

DONNA. It's just me. *(Holds up her phone.)* Phone call.

JOANNE. Where did he wander off?

DONNA. *(As she looks through paperwork:)* I think he's around.

> **JOANNE** *removes a little yellow Post-It Note from her glasses case.*

JOANNE. *(Reads it:)* "Glasses." Our apartment is filled with these. Hundreds of little notes in Righty's messy handwriting. Table, Toilet, Knife. *(Has a little trouble getting through the following:)* We have an oil painting of a sunset. Righty stuck a Post-It on it. "Sunset." Can you imagine? I found a note that said "I love you," stuck on a can of bug spray. I don't know what he was trying to say with that.

DONNA. That he loved you.

JOANNE. I hope so.

DONNA. That all sounds really hard. Why don't we see if we can get you some help.

JOANNE. That's very kind of you. But your idea of help seems to just be money.

DONNA. Well, maybe we can help in some other ways.

JOANNE. I don't think you understand that there are things beyond helping, here.

DONNA. Of course. I can't imagine. But I should...this is a difficult... *(Very brief pause.)* It's just one grave, just one occupant, that Mr. Morse arranged for.

JOANNE. I'm sorry?

DONNA. There's not a place for you here. To be laid to rest.

JOANNE. You don't know that. How could you know that?

She picks up a biscuit.

DONNA. I've been checking deeds and titles and leases going back a hundred years.

JOANNE. Why would you tell me that?

She puts the biscuit back in the package.

DONNA. It's the truth. And for your own planning. *(Lays out a map of the area, including Briarwood Cemetery.)* This is the plot grid here. Righty's was the last available place.

JOANNE. Yes, thank you. *(Looks at the map for a moment.)* He probably forgot.

DONNA. He got his own paperwork done correctly. *(Brief pause.)* He probably forgot.

JOANNE. You'll have to look again under the name St. Onge. My maiden name is St. Onge.

DONNA. That's a memorable name.

JOANNE. Thank you.

DONNA. I mean I think I'd remember it.

JOANNE. Well, I'm... We shall certainly have to have a talk about that, won't we. This, the... *(Sad and unguarded:)* He didn't forget. He just thought about himself. And where does that leave me for all eternity? Or for the next ninety-nine years? Maybe I should just accept your offer, whatever it is.

DONNA. I believe it's really very generous.

JOANNE. *(Looks at the map again. She points. Very quietly:)* That's the other place Righty loves. The pasture. Whenever he disappears, he's either here or there.

DONNA. Oh yeah? *(Looks at the map.)* What's that? "The Cabot Pasture."

JOANNE. He's got his gravesite here, and the Cabot Pasture. That's practically his whole world. And you want to take away half of it – you want to take away his final resting place here.

DONNA. What I want is to help you enjoy your life.

JOANNE. And do you enjoy your life? *(Very brief pause.)* That wasn't fair. *(Looks over the cemetery.)* I guess he could still go over to the pasture. He does love it. There's blackberries growing all over everything. It's right back through there.

DONNA. It sounds beautiful.

JOANNE. It is. Who owns it?

DONNA. I don't know.

JOANNE. That's not getting paved over, is it?

DONNA. No, no plans for that. Nothing I know about.

JOANNE. I hope not. I don't know what he'd do.

DONNA. He's really grounded in these places, isn't he.

JOANNE. *(Referring to the biscuits:)* May I have another cookie?

DONNA. Please. Take the whole package.

JOANNE. Maybe I'll do this? *(Puts the package in her bag.)* For later?

DONNA. Of course.

JOANNE. I don't think about it like Righty, but, I really could imagine being buried there, in the pasture.

DONNA. You both could. If Righty gives up his place here.

JOANNE. And since I never had a place here to begin with. *(Brief pause.)* Thank you. I'm sure it wasn't easy to tell me that.

DONNA. No. I'm sorry.

JOANNE. I'm not going to sign anything today.

DONNA. Of course. Here's my card, call any time.

JOANNE. I might not sign anything ever.

DONNA. Of course.

She takes out an index card and writes on it.

DONNA. I'm going to write a figure on this card here.

JOANNE. *(While chewing:)* What fun.

    DONNA *slides the index card over toward* **JOANNE**, *who glances at it without picking it up.*

DONNA. *(Very brief pause.)* Someone offered you a house?

JOANNE. What?

DONNA. As part of a deal, for Righty's spot?

JOANNE. Oh, I don't know – we get twenty phone calls a day. Home slipper delivery, medical alert bracelets. There might have been something about a house, but it was piles of forms to fill out and all kinds of costs. They wanted us to pay for an inspection.

DONNA. That sounds like a hassle.

JOANNE. Well, but it *was* a house. I have all their information, somewhere.

DONNA. It's really important to you, getting out of your apartment. Maybe that's something we can look at.

JOANNE. It's my last dream. But everything's always getting bought and re-sold and all the prices keep going up.

DONNA. Well, we know there's a lot of interest and I believe our offer reflects that.

    She pushes the index card closer to **JOANNE**.

Would you like to take a look?

JOANNE. Just one minute. I need to adjust to all of this.

    She takes a breath and closes her eyes.

DONNA. Of course. And I'm going to keep digging around to see if we might find some other options here. *(In a slightly louder voice, toward where Righty exited:)* I understand it's difficult for everyone. I just want you both to feel –

JOANNE. *(Interrupting:)* – Yes, thank you. I'd like to be alone.

DONNA. Yeah, of course. Bye. Thank you.

She exits. **JOANNE** *sits still for a moment more. Then she takes a quick peek at the figure and her face very subtly suggests it's a generous offer. She closes her eyes again.*

RIGHTY. *(Enters.)* There's no paper towels. Were you sleeping?

JOANNE. Do you remember what you told me about this place?

RIGHTY. It's morbid.

JOANNE. That's what *I* told *you*. But remember, about your plans? For both of us.

RIGHTY. We'll be side by side.

JOANNE. And you arranged that?

RIGHTY. I talked with them later, separate.

JOANNE. You're sure?

RIGHTY. Didn't I ask you if you liked your middle name?

JOANNE. That was for this?

RIGHTY. Did they call? *(Brief pause.)* I know I can't get around like I used to.

JOANNE. You do fine. *(Very brief pause.)* Richard, I think there's a way out of this.

RIGHTY. No, leave it like it is. I finally feel calm, you know? Please, Joanne. Thank you.

JOANNE. *(Brief pause.)* What do you want for lunch?

RIGHTY. Grilled cheese. *(Picks up the index card.)* Whoa. Who left all this money lying here?

JOANNE. That's just a piece of paper with a number on it.

RIGHTY. That's what money is.

JOANNE. *(Little smile.)* You're very sharp, today.

RIGHTY. *(Quietly:)* Someone's going to pay for it.

JOANNE. *(Not having heard:)* What's that?

RIGHTY. Should we...hmm. What was I saying? Oh. Let's have tomato on it.

Lights change. Nighttime sounds. An animal scurries past.

Scene Four

Late morning, a week later. The graveyard. One of the older graves has been removed. There is a patch of new, upturned dirt in a neat rectangle. Now there is only one last old gravestone, and Righty's new gravestone. Near the gazebo, a long folding table has been set up, along with some chairs. Some photos and basic architectural models are on the table. An easel is set off to the side. **DONNA** *and* **GREY** *sit at the table, working.* **TIM** *is on the other side, on his cell phone.)*

TIM. *(Into phone:)* Not a problem, Mr. Neubatten. Of course: "Paul." Well, right now, I'm looking at about twenty people going over every inch of the whole project. *(Brief pause.)* Well, Paul, I'm sure every graveyard used to be another graveyard. And there's always the whole Save the Lemmings crowd. *(Brief pause.)* I know. Because lemmings actually – right, that's what made it a joke. *(Brief pause.)* Agreed. It's no time for jokes. We'll deal with this and break ground in two weeks, you have my word. *(Very brief pause.)* Yeah, I can hold. *(Rests his head in his hands. To* **DONNA***:)* Can you get my lunch. It's in the car. *(Into phone:)* What? Oh, hi, Teddy. I didn't know you were on this call.

    DONNA *exits.*

(Into phone, eagerly:) Yup, I'm here. Sure, Paul, we can talk whenever you – hello? *(Hangs up. Quietly:)* Fucking shithead.

GREY. Bad news?

TIM. You worked for him, right?

GREY. I did the Apiary at the Brentmoor Estate. His wife Sonya is really interested in bees and so that's how –

TIM. – He thinks he's so smart.

GREY. He's pretty smart.

DONNA *enters and hands* **TIM** *a take-out bag.*

DONNA. Here you go.

TIM. Neubatten's not coming today.

DONNA. Oh, no. Why?

TIM. He was talking about this being a sacred site. *(Looking at* **GREY***:)* Which seems like something you'd say.

GREY. Yeah, it really does.

TIM. *(Very brief pause.)* And then there was some environmental stuff.

DONNA. Well, he'll like the environmental impact study I'm doing. I just have to tweak a few more numbers. And the sacred-site rumors have been around forever.

TIM. He's called five times in the last week. I want to just tell the guy, "Hey, stupid moneybags, why don't you go fucking die, you piece-of-shit idiot." But I don't, because I'm a professional. And I need his money. *(Very brief pause.)* Whatever I am inside, whatever I'm feeling, all the world sees is a man eating his lunch.

> *He opens the bag and takes out a plastic container of food. He looks through the bag.*

DONNA. It's pretty amazing, the way you keep your feelings and your work life –

TIM. – God-fucking-damn it, did they forget the cockfucking – no, sorry, here they are. *(Takes out some chopsticks. Places them properly in his hand.)* Chopsticks. When in Rome, right? Behold, I am a man eating his lunch. Anyway, give me an update.

DONNA. Of course. *(Quickly checking notes:)* Actually, Grey was able to –

> **TIM** *takes a bite of food.*

TIM. – Ooh, hot hot hot.

> *He deals with it, either drinking something, fanning his mouth, or spitting the food out.*

DONNA. You okay?

GREY. We got a Disposition of Remains permit for that last old grave there, so that's all done.

DONNA. Next-of-kin was a very distant relative who was happy to have some ashes and the standard payment. The cremation was done at Houseman's Funeral Home.

TIM. Great. Teamwork. The public and private sectors. Two really great sectors. *(Takes another bite.)* Did you pay Houseman's on the company card?

DONNA. Yeah.

TIM. I'm hitting my limit on that one, so switch it to my personal card.

>*He hands* **DONNA** *a credit card.*

DONNA. Yeah? Maxing out the credit cards. This is the big leagues.

TIM. It is.

DONNA. I'll email them now. *(Begins to type on her phone.)* That last old grave is still in process. No relatives, no trace of anyone, but I think we're good.

>*With take-out food in hand,* **TIM** *walks over to take a closer look at this last old gravestone.* **DONNA** *types credit card info into her phone.* **TIM** *pushes away some weeds and reads the partly-eroded inscription:*

TIM. "Louise Dagenhart. The Universe is fatal." Sounds like a real party girl. *(Heads back to the table.)* And what about Morse here? The guy who hasn't died yet.

DONNA. *(Still finishing email:)* Well, it's kind of an emotional situation.

TIM. Not for me, it isn't.

>*He takes another bite.*

DONNA. The good news is, his wife is on board. Joanne. We'll do the payment, and she asked about the Cabot Pasture.

TIM. The what?

DONNA. The Cabot Pasture. That little piece of land back there.

TIM. Oh, right. Why'd she ask about that? What, she wants to raise mosquitos?

DONNA. Her husband likes sitting over there. And since this place is getting torn up, she wanted him to still have a special place to go. I think she feels guilty about not honoring his final wishes and all that.

TIM. Okay, yeah, the Cabot Pasture. It's been on the market forever. I think the listing agent is here in town, so that should be a snap. Tell her they can have it.

DONNA. I met with her, again, last night. You told me to get it done.

TIM. And it sounds like you're getting it done.

DONNA. I am. One last thing, I said we'd give them a house.

TIM. *(Little laugh.)* Well, you shouldn't have, because we won't be doing that. Just raise the bid. Go another fifty percent, max. In increments, though. Little increments. *(Picks something out of his food using chopsticks.)* What is that? *(Flings it away.)* Water chestnut. What is the point of a water chestnut?

DONNA. The home is really important. Trust me. Other people offered one, but they set it up in a really confusing way.

TIM. Who else is interested? It's a fucking hole in the stupid ground. We can't void his lease? You went through every option?

DONNA. Backwards and forwards, yeah. They live in a tiny little depressing one-bedroom. They're not budging. She isn't.

TIM. *(Brief pause.)* Dagenhart or whatever isn't going to be any trouble, right?

DONNA. No.

TIM. So we take care of this and we're done?

DONNA. Yeah.

TIM. *(Brief pause. He thinks.)* I have a two-bedroom Cape on Janeway Street that's sort of in limbo. It's actually a pretty sweet little place.

DONNA. Oh, that's perfect. You're incredible. Thank you.

TIM. All right. This actually works out. Everybody wins. *(Very brief pause.)* Did you talk to Neubatten?

DONNA. No. Why would *I* talk to him?

TIM. I'm just wondering why he suddenly seemed skittish.

DONNA. I haven't talked with anybody.

TIM. Is that a new blouse?

DONNA. What? No, actually.

TIM. Hmm. *(To* **GREY***:)* Why are you still here? He's not coming.

GREY. No, I know. Maybe I can help, since I'm already here. You know, brainstorm with Donna.

TIM. Great. Please. *(Makes a small gesture.)* Brainstorm.

GREY. What?

TIM. I wonder if I should've gotten the fried rice.

GREY. You know what, I'm going to work on my painting. I'm doing a painting of this place.

TIM. This is the last of the roadblocks, right? Morse?

DONNA. Like I said, she's ready to sign off.

TIM. Since you very shrewdly gave her a house in exchange for a tiny rectangle of dirt. Does she have power-of-attorney?

DONNA. No.

TIM. So make sure they both sign.

DONNA. She definitely takes the lead on everything.

She steps away, dials.

Joanne? It's Donna, at Tyson Properties. I just have a second, but I wanted to call with some great news. I just spoke with Mr. Tyson…

She continues, out of earshot.

TIM. *(To* **GREY***:)* You're all right with this thing moving forward?

GREY. It's a balance. Business and the environment.

TIM. Yes, it's a balance. Good man.

DONNA. *(Enters.)* They're thrilled. Thank you, Tim. You're a sweetheart.

TIM. Do it as an "As Is" sale, and just put a dollar for the purchase price. *(Very brief pause.)* We really have a chance to make the future. *(Gestures toward graves.)* Unlike these clowns. You don't hear skeletons and remains being called clowns, very much, do you. It's interesting.

DONNA. It is. I'll make sure he signs. It all just takes a little work.

TIM. Most jobs have some work involved, that's why it's called – dot dot dot, wait for it...*trabajo.* *(To* **GREY***:)* You weren't expecting a Spanish word, but you were wrong!

GREY. *(Hasn't been paying attention.)* What's that?

DONNA. I just want to make sure that – I mean, Righty, he's a fragile person facing mortality, in the middle of losing his faculties.

TIM. Everyone has to face that stuff, and, if they're lucky, they don't have to face it with all their faculties.

DONNA. Something about this place spoke to his soul, it made him less scared. Which, I wish I had that kind of connection. Almost like him being buried here is going to protect the place. And the place'll protect him.

TIM. Believe – whatever you're talking about – I get it. I'm not some caricature whose only purpose here is to help deface a sacred site and put in a cold-storage facility and a fully-modernized truck bay, although I do really want to do that.

DONNA. No, of course.

TIM. I have feelings and ideas, just like everyone.

DONNA. Just like me.

TIM. Sure. You, too. But at a certain point, philosophy and thoughts don't matter. Life is getting rid of dead stuff to make room for living stuff. That's what cells do, that's what the ancient Egyptians did, the Romans, and that's what we do. I don't see you writing any of this down.

DONNA. No, it's good. Good stuff. That's true, about life.

GREY. "Those who don't learn from history –

TIM. – The thing I always hated about that quote is that the people who DO learn from history are probably doomed to repeat it, too. *(To **DONNA**:)* Let's get this all done, and then we'll take a trip to the Caribbean and pay for everything with little shells. We'll get a disposable camera, they're amazing – you can completely cut out the middleman and all the posing, and just throw the thing straight in the trash.

DONNA. *(As she's making a note:)* Oh, I could use a vacation. Shells. Fun.

TIM. *(Looking in the bag:)* You have to be fucking kidding – where's my shit-assing tiramisu? *(Composes himself.)* I was looking forward to that.

DONNA. I told them twice. They didn't put it in there?

TIM. It's fine. First you get Neubatten to panic and then you mess up my dessert order.

DONNA. I even had them read it back to me.

TIM. I'm sure it was just an honest mistake. I accused you of two things, though.

DONNA. No, I said I never... I already said I didn't talk to him.

TIM. Okay. Now, if you'll excuse me, I believe I'll go urinate into the hole where Franklin Pierce was buried.

DONNA. You mean his cousin.

TIM. Does that make it sound better?

GREY. They have facilities here.

*(**TIM** strolls out of sight.)*

DONNA. *(Looking at her phone, quietly:)* Goddamn it.

GREY. Sometimes these things just fall apart on their own.

DONNA. Oh, phew. Thank you.

GREY. *(Brief pause.)* What do you see in him?

DONNA. *(Still mainly working with her phone:)* Excuse me? Who the fuck are you? Seriously. I'm not being rhetorical or metaphorical.

GREY. I'm sorry.

DONNA. My life is not exactly brimming with options.

GREY. Okay, but you might reconsider your commitment, here.

DONNA. What do you mean? Do you know something?

GREY. I'm just not sure the guy who just urinated into someone's eternal resting place is the star you want to be hitching your wagon to.

DONNA. He's not how he always acts and talks and seems. He's giving that old couple a house, for God's sakes. Just so you know, we're just two busy people. He's getting divorced and we have some plans, but, we're just having fun. It's not serious.

GREY. He said it was.

DONNA. He did?

> **GREY** *nods a very small "no."*

Okay. Very good.

GREY. Sorry.

DONNA. Go ahead, make fun of my stupid life choices.

GREY. I'm sorry. It's, just, maybe there's other choices you could make.

DONNA. Really? Maybe you could help me? This is so amazing, it's taken almost two minutes, but, finally, another fucking man is here to tell me what choices I should make.

GREY. I'm... Yeah, I'm sorry. *(Brief pause.)* I'm just surprised. You're so... I don't know.

DONNA. No, you don't. *(Brief pause.)* What?

GREY. I wasn't going to –. So, I did the garden design at the Kingfisher Armory.

DONNA. That was me. That was my whole project.

GREY. I know.

DONNA. Almost four years of my life. That's right, you did the gardens. I read about you, while I was living in my aunt's basement.

GREY. I started right after you were done.

DONNA. "Done." I got replaced a few months before we opened by someone's fucking son-in-law.

GREY. I didn't mention it in case it was a sore spot.

DONNA. Thanks. But then you did mention it. And it is a huge sore spot.

GREY. But it all started with you and your letter to the paper.

DONNA. "Let us now praise famous buildings."

GREY. With the restaurant and the stores, and the sustainability. But mainly making people feel proud of that place, of the original building. And connected to it. I love the panels that show the changes over the years.

DONNA. I found some really old audio recordings of kids laughing and playing, from back when it was an orphanage. It was my idea to have that playing in one of the common areas.

GREY. I know, I love it. It's kind of haunting and kind of fun. The whole place, it just makes you feel good, being there.

DONNA. Really?

GREY. My grandma goes, just to hang out. It's like the mall for her and her eighty-year-old friends.

DONNA. That's...thanks for telling me that. I really loved working on that thing.

GREY. So, that's the only reason I was... I'm sorry for butting into your business.

DONNA. That's all right. *(Brief pause.)* I thought my life was really going to start, after that.

A brief, sad pause.

TIM *enters.*

TIM. What sort of moment am I walking into?

DONNA. Nothing. A normal moment.

GREY. Donna, what kind of things are you imagining here?

TIM. *(To* **GREY***:)* Could you leave us alone, for a minute.

GREY. Now?

TIM. Thanks.

GREY. *(Hesitantly starts to leave.)* You know what, I'm going to take my stuff. I have a meeting.

TIM. We just need a few minutes.

GREY. *(Referring to his easel:)* Will this be okay here?

TIM. That I don't know.

> **GREY** *exits with his bag, leaving the easel.* **TIM** *starts to read a document.* **DONNA** *watches him and waits.*

DONNA. Did you want to talk about something?

> *Sound of text on* **TIM**'s *phone, which he begins to read.*

TIM. Not really. *(He's distracted with phone.)* The deed for the Janeway Street house is at the office.

DONNA. She is so happy. And I'm really glad he'll be taken care of. You're doing something that's going to be profitable *and* kind.

TIM. Very profitable. Our fee is a percentage of the total initial cost, plus an interest in the ongoing business.

DONNA. Wow. Wow.

TIM. You can put everything in her name, his name, whatever they prefer.

DONNA. Okay that's great – I'll check what she wants.

TIM. It's currently in dispute as to whether the house has to be demolished, but that'll take time.

DONNA. Wait, what?

TIM. It's fine. It's to make room for the new police department building. Which might not even happen. *(Working his phone:)* I'm not giving anyone a house.

DONNA. You said you would.

TIM. No, *you* said I would. Tell them two things. "Welcome to your new home." And, "You don't have to do a thing." Both, at the time, will be a hundred percent true.

DONNA. And then a wrecking ball comes through the window?

TIM. No, come on. They'll get a notice to vacate, if it even happens. And if it doesn't, they take care of some code violations and the place is theirs. Or they knock it down and sell the land.

Sound of a snapping twig. **GREY** *appears.*

Well, hello. Is that the sound of a snapping twig I hear?

GREY. I know. Classic. *(Looking around:)* I lost my pen.

TIM. What kind is it?

GREY. Nothing special but it's my favorite.

TIM. Hmm – now where did that guy's favorite pen go? I'll keep an eye out.

GREY. Here it is.

He picks it up and exits.

TIM. Oh good.

He watches **GREY** *leave.*

What's his deal?

DONNA. I don't know.

TIM. You've gotta watch your back. And your front, and your sides.

DONNA. *(A little sadly:)* What if you just want to look at the world?

TIM. Come on, smile. You did really great work here. Those folks'll be okay. They're getting money, the Cabot Pasture, and some free rent for a little while. If you're going to break some eggs, you might as well make an omelette. We're doing this. Okay? You and me.

DONNA. Okay.

They kiss.

TIM. Personal question – can you get the table and chairs? And put the model in my office.

DONNA. Yeah. Hey, I haven't eaten, and I was thinking –

TIM. – Sure, good idea, go grab a bite.

>*He hands her some money.*

I gotta run.

>*He exits.*

>**DONNA** *packs up her bag, considers picking up the model, etc., but then decides to leave. She dials her phone. As she's exiting:*

DONNA. *(Into phone:)* Joanne.

>*Lights.*

Scene Five

The graveyard. Dusk. The next day. Some gentle woodland sounds. The architectural model and other materials are still there. **GREY** *is working at an easel, angled so we don't see his painting. He works quietly, seeming to commune with the setting.*

RIGHTY *enters. He looks at the model.*

GREY. That's for a development project here.

RIGHTY. It's like a toy train set. Lionel trains.

GREY. Are you here to visit? I can give you some privacy.

RIGHTY. No. I like coming here.

GREY. Me too. People don't really understand, do they. How special a place can be.

RIGHTY. Is that a painting?

GREY. Yeah.

RIGHTY. What's it for?

GREY. Just, I want to remember this place.

RIGHTY. I do too.

GREY. So, you know about the plans? The development?

RIGHTY. *(Smiling and shaking his head:)* People and their plans.

GREY. Yeah, you're right. There's probably five different graveyards under this one, all of them all filled up with people planning something or other.

RIGHTY. *(A little unsettled by the remark:)* Yeah. *(Very brief pause.)* Can I look?

GREY. Sure. It's not finished yet.

> **RIGHTY** *comes around and looks for a moment. He moves on, continuing to look around, without comment or expression.*
>
> *An awkward moment, from* **GREY**'s *perspective.*

Nothing?

RIGHTY. What?

GREY. No comment on the painting? Never mind.

RIGHTY. You said it wasn't finished. If I had a comment, I guess I'd say, "Yup."

GREY. Okay. Fair enough.

RIGHTY. It's good you're doing that. To help people with the beauty.

GREY. *(Looks around and soaks in his surroundings.)* And it's not going to be around much longer.

RIGHTY. Why not?

GREY. Progress, right? Because I guess the world needs noise.

> **RIGHTY** *looks at his gravesite.* **GREY** *continues painting. He gestures toward the gravesite.*

That one's probably getting dug up.

RIGHTY. I thought these things were forever.

GREY. You wouldn't believe all the wheeling and dealing.

RIGHTY. About this?

GREY. People getting cheated, big business contracts, all this noisy stuff happening, over such a quiet place.

RIGHTY. Who's getting cheated?

GREY. *(Tries to let it go.)* Oh, who knows.

RIGHTY. People, huh? People being people to other people.

GREY. Some old couple is getting pushed into a condemned property, in exchange for their place out here.

RIGHTY. Condemned?

GREY. Well, not officially condemned. It's all a big legal mess.

RIGHTY. What's the old couple going to do?

GREY. My friend is working on it. I think she'll make it as right as she can. I don't know how right that'll be, though.

RIGHTY. What?

GREY. It's none of my business but isn't there a saying, "There's no such thing as a free two-bedroom house on Janeway Street"?

RIGHTY. No. It's "free lunch." No free lunch. The thing you said isn't a saying.

> **DONNA** *enters, unseen. She stands off to the side.* **RIGHTY** *looks at the model.*

RIGHTY. It's pretty ugly. What is it, a little factory?

GREY. It's a distribution center.

RIGHTY. I like the little trees.

GREY. There should be more.

RIGHTY. So put more.

GREY. The final design is up to a guy named Paul Neubatten. Although I'm doing some work for his wife Sonya, so maybe I can get his ear. You know what she told me the other day?

RIGHTY. I don't know who she is. How could I know what she told –

GREY. – No, of course. She told me I don't take enough joy or panic in things. She said, "Feel one or both but not neither." I was telling her I want to leave a mark, a gentle mark, some sign I lived.

RIGHTY. I'd like that too.

GREY. Anyway, she had some other ideas. Part of me wants to let everyone lie here in peace, all the layers of cemeteries and bodies, but the more I visit, the more I feel them all kind of cheering me on. "Come on, Grey. You can do it. Get involved. Plenty of time for peace and quiet. Participate."

> **RIGHTY** *nods.*

RIGHTY. There used to be a green trash can, right there.

GREY. *(A little disappointed in that response:)* Yeah?

DONNA. *(Appears. To* **RIGHTY***:)* Well, look who it is.

RIGHTY. Hello.

DONNA. We have to stop meeting like this.

RIGHTY. Okay.

DONNA. No, I'm kidding. Has Grey here been boring you to tears?

RIGHTY. A bit, yes.

DONNA. I just saw your wife.

RIGHTY. Joanne.

DONNA. So, how're you doing?

RIGHTY. I'm good.

He lies down in front of his gravestone, where he'd be buried.

Here I am. As advertised.

GREY. *(Mouthing the words:)* He's that guy?

DONNA *nods.*

DONNA. *(Gently:)* Mr. Morse...you all right? *(Brief pause.)* You taking a rest?

RIGHTY. Yup. Participate. *(Sits up. Quietly:)* I'm the worst person you ever met.

DONNA. *(With sympathy:)* No, no. That's really common. My grandfather got so depressed. He did not "go gently," if you can picture that. I'm sure you're not a bad person. But just in case, let's do something good.

She takes out a contract.

RIGHTY. Is this to take care of Joanne?

DONNA. Yes, and of you, too. There's the date, so you can just sign right there.

RIGHTY. You can see me, right?

DONNA. Of course.

RIGHTY. I read in the paper where the elderly are called "The Invisible People."

DONNA. *(Referring to the contract:)* This'll be great, just to be safe. Joanne already signed.

RIGHTY. Joanne used to be on my side.

DONNA. She still is.

RIGHTY. She told me to remember something. What was it?

He thinks, and looks at **GREY.**

GREY. Your blood type?

RIGHTY. No, but that's good.

DONNA. *(Looking around, taking it in:)* It really is a special spot. I just want you to know, I feel it too.

GREY. Really?

DONNA. Yes, really.

RIGHTY. *(Remembering:)* I'm supposed to ask about the pasture.

DONNA. Yes! The Cabot Pasture. What a peaceful spot. Guess what? Mr. Tyson has secured that for you. That'll be all yours.

RIGHTY. That's another place for me to go. I come here if I'm worried. I go there when I'm sad.

DONNA. Joanne really wanted to make sure you felt cared for. She really fought for that land, the Cabot land.

RIGHTY. *(Looks around.)* I'm glad this'll still be here, too.

DONNA. Well, but it'll be different.

RIGHTY. No, this place'll never change.

DONNA. Mm-hmm. And you'll also have the house on Janeway Street. So you can get out of that cramped apartment.

RIGHTY. You're really taking care of us.

>   **DONNA** *hands him the contract and a pen.*

What's your name again?

DONNA. Donna. And you're Richard "Righty" Morse.

>   **RIGHTY** *looks at her.*

You know that. Is that a nickname?

>   **RIGHTY** *signs. She points to another line on another page.*

And that next page, where the little sticker is.

>   **RIGHTY** *signs. She turns to another page.*

And that last one.

RIGHTY. My hand is going to fall off.

>   *He signs.*

DONNA. Wonderful! Congratulations.

>   *She puts the contract away.*

RIGHTY. I feel like smiling.

He is not smiling.

DONNA. I do too. Thank you. Thank you so much.

RIGHTY. Okay – bye bye, I guess. Now, where am I going?

DONNA. Home? I can give you a lift.

RIGHTY. I can walk, I like the walk. *(To* **GREY***:)* I think you have a good perspective. You have a good, um... perspective.

GREY. Thanks. You too.

DONNA. Bye, Mr. Morse.

>   **RIGHTY** *exits.*

Art critic, all of a sudden. He's a trip, huh? *(Very quietly, to herself:)* Yes!

GREY. Happy?

DONNA. I am. *(Brief pause.)* What?

GREY. I just hope they're being treated right.

DONNA. One thing at a time, here, okay?

> *She happily begins packing things up. The sun is setting. A gorgeous sky.*

I've felt that thing – wanting to make a mark. To leave some sign. I heard what you said.

GREY. Oh. I actually said quite a lot, today.

DONNA. Yeah? I stopped by over at the Armory this morning. I love the bridge of flowers. And the birdhouses. I always did but it was fun to look again, knowing you did it.

GREY. Thanks.

DONNA. I didn't know you were working for Mrs. Neubatten.

GREY. It's just a proposal, at this point. A sort of pergola, with a little pond.

DONNA. Still. Good person to know. I'd love to meet her sometime.

GREY. She's always off somewhere, flying around.

DONNA. No, I'm sure.

There's a bottle of wine among the supplies.
DONNA *pours herself a paper cup of it.*

DONNA. Care to... I'm going to have some of this. I think I earned it.

She drinks.

GREY. I actually could use a drink. Is there another...

He finds a paper cup, pours some wine, has a sip.

Ah...red.

DONNA. *(Very drily:)* I didn't know you knew so much about wines. *(Sips.)* It's all happening. *(Looks around.)* This place is actually kind of sexy. Have you ever done it in a graveyard?

GREY. If by "it" you mean "cry," I have. Twice.

DONNA. I didn't mean cry.

GREY. Then, no.

DONNA. I meant: close on a massive real estate deal. No, I'm kidding, I meant sexual intercourse.

GREY. I'm just double-checking I heard correctly, here: *sexual* intercourse?

DONNA. Exactly. It's intercourse, but, how can I say this, it's sexual.

GREY. Is this flirting?

DONNA. You're such a nerd.

GREY. Was *that* flirting?

DONNA. Don't get the wrong idea, here, or the right one.

GREY. Got it. No ideas. I'll start right away.

DONNA. Life is real, isn't it. Life and death are real.

GREY. You feeling pretty good?

DONNA. I am. *(Raises her cup.)* To me. Making it all happen.

GREY. *(A toast of his own, as he looks at the cemetery:)* To earthworms and mushrooms, also making it all happen.

DONNA. Yuck.

GREY. *(A toast he shares with* **DONNA***:)* To paper cups and red-colored wine.

DONNA. There you go.

> *They drink.*

Do you really hear people saying things here?

GREY. Sort of.

DONNA. I don't get a lot of encouragement from the actual world, from the…yeah, from the real world.

GREY. No?

> *They move toward each other. An "almost" sort of moment.*

DONNA. A graveyard, of all places. *(To the last old gravestone:)* Hello, Miss Louise Dagenhart. The Universe is fatal? So says you.

> **TIM** *enters.*

TIM. What are you two doing here? This stuff got left out here overnight? Ooh, wine. What are we celebrating? I hope something.

> *He pours some wine and drinks.*
>
> **DONNA** *gets the contract out and gives it to him.*

DONNA. Read it and weep.

TIM. You're kidding me! Is this what I think it is?

> *He kisses her.*

DONNA. I just kept smiling and handing him the pen.

GREY. I didn't know who he was.

DONNA. I feel eight miles high.

TIM. You should. Yee-haw.

GREY. We chatted quite a bit.

DONNA. We'll move that last one, Dagenhart over there, to a storage facility. I want to get a crew here as soon as possible.

TIM. Yes, do it. Give Houseman's a call. Neubatten is going to tour the site in a few days. *(Looking over the contract:)* You probably had to push pretty hard.

DONNA. I stayed focused.

TIM. *(With a little glee:)* Did he get a little mad?

DONNA. Oh, I don't know, maybe a little. Why?

TIM. *(Plainly:)* Because on the dotted line here, where you're supposed to put your signature, he just wrote, "Fuck you, Donna."

DONNA. What?

TIM. With a little smiley face inside the O in your name.

> *He flips through the pages to check the other "signatures." Whatever is written there makes him smile a very small, rueful smile.*

You got outwitted by a very confused man.

DONNA. That's not – no. Let me see.

> **TIM** *hands it back to her. Checks the time. He's moved on entirely.*

TIM. I was driving by and I saw your car. Get this stuff back, all right?

DONNA. I'll get them to sign everything. He doesn't know what he's doing.

TIM. Oh, *he* doesn't know what he's doing? All I asked was this one thing – pay two old people a bunch of money to sign a practically worthless piece of paper. I guess I'll have to take care of it myself.

GREY. I think he's really confused.

TIM. Thanks, Grey.

GREY. Who knows what crazy idea he got in his head. Donna was really good with him. I can try to talk to him.

DONNA. I don't need help.

TIM. Yeah. Please. Obviously, she can do it herself. *(Looks at **GREY**'s painting.)* The fine arts aren't my exact thing, but, looking good.

GREY. Thanks.

TIM. *(To* **DONNA***:)* So Victoria and I seem to have reconciled. *(To* **GREY***:)* My wife. *(To* **DONNA***:)* So...yeah. This ship has sailed, I guess is what I'm saying. There was a ship, admittedly kind of a crappy ship, and the ship has sailed.

> *He exits.*
>
> *A pause.*

GREY. I think this is good, actually. It gives us some time to –

DONNA. – Please, don't. "Us"?

GREY. What got into that guy? Mr. Morse? You know?

DONNA. *(Looks over the graveyard.)* There's fourteen dead people for every living person on Earth. They can't all still be buried. The ground would be overflowing. But they're somewhere. Out of fifteen people, I'm the sucker, the one stuck here, above ground, uncremated.

GREY. No. Hey, Donna –

DONNA. *(Screams:)* – Auuuughhhh!

> **GREY** *gets his easel and paint box.*

GREY. I'll leave you alone.

DONNA. Thank you.

GREY. Call me, okay? If there's anything.

DONNA. There isn't anything.

> **GREY** *exits.*
>
> **DONNA** *packs up some stuff. She's trying not to cry but not succeeding. She goes into the gazebo, lies down, and lies there holding herself.*
>
> **RIGHTY** *enters. He looks at the model for a moment, looks around. His phone rings. He sort of slowly and clumsily opens the phone and answers the call.*

RIGHTY. *(Into phone.)* Hello? Oh, good – hey, Mike. Yeah, I think that's best – anything that comes in, put it straight into a sweep account, please, which, that'll be there to cover the interest, with a little left over for fees or whatever. *(Brief pause.)* Yeah, just another month or two, and I think I can pay it down to zero. I had to play a little hardball – kind of a weird hardball/softball mix, actually, but it's coming together. *(Brief pause.)* Jo is great, thank you for asking. Okay. Yeah, I think she's going to be really excited.

He turns to find **DONNA** *staring at him.*

(Into phone:) I'm not supposed to use the phone. Bye bye.

He ends the call. Looks at the model.

DONNA. Who were you talking to?

RIGHTY. A little toy train set.

DONNA. It's an architectural model.

RIGHTY. Oh.

DONNA. To whom – if I may ask – who were you just talking to?

RIGHTY. That was…um. Who was that? My doctor.

DONNA *stares into his eyes.*

DONNA. Oh my God, don't tell me, please do not tell me.

RIGHTY. Okay.

DONNA. Were you pretending?

RIGHTY. Was I…?

DONNA. Are you faking that you have Alzheimer's?

RIGHTY. *(Very brief pause.)* It's a long story.

DONNA. I would fucking hope so.

RIGHTY. Bring everything over tonight, we'll sign whatever you need.

DONNA. Like you signed it before? You humiliated me. Is Joanne in on this? *(Brief pause.)* Oh, my God.

RIGHTY. I was wrong, I'm sorry, and I realize it now.

DONNA. What you realize is you don't want to be caught living this disgusting, heinous lie. *(Very brief pause.)* Was it something you noticed – people being too trusting, too empathetic? Were people taking disease and aging too seriously and so you decided something had to be done?

RIGHTY. It took a few steps to get here.

DONNA. Give me one. You're sitting there with Joanne, your wife of many decades. What's the very first thought?

RIGHTY. You wouldn't understand. It's complicated.

DONNA. Try me.

RIGHTY. I wanted a little more "me time."

DONNA. Oh my God.

RIGHTY. That didn't come out right.

DONNA. You're the worst person I've ever – *(Very brief pause.)* Which you told me. In those exact words.

RIGHTY. You were perfectly comfortable sticking some old couple into a condemned property. A couple whose life you believed was ravaged by disease. You were very happy turning a wife against her husband's dying wishes.

DONNA. And I'm ashamed of that. And, yes, there are some legal issues with the house. Lucky you were faking.

RIGHTY. But maybe I'll actually get some disease just like it and then who's going to be laughing?

DONNA. No one?

RIGHTY. *(Realizing and agreeing:)* Probably no one. Actually, that's true.

DONNA. *(Brief pause.)* I have to tell your wife, right now.

RIGHTY. Please don't. I'll tell her everything, I promise, after we get our finances settled. I know you didn't want to lie to us. I know you tried to help us, before you eventually didn't. Let me tell. It'll still hurt her, but at least I can try to explain.

DONNA. *(Quietly:)* I cannot believe the things people do. Me included. Me included.

RIGHTY. We aren't getting rich here. I always loved this place and I heard it was being developed. At first I got angry, and then I thought I could make some money.

And the Alzheimer's got us into a help program that we really needed. Because Joanne is going to need a lot of help. Do you know about her situation?

DONNA. That she's married to a man who pretends to have Alzheimer's?

RIGHTY. No, her health.

DONNA. Oh, no! Does she have Alzheimer's? It's such a heartbreaking disease.

RIGHTY. I tried to take care of us and I made mistakes. I can understand you not believing anything I say.

DONNA. And there we are – period. *(Brief pause.)* Here's what I know: Joanne is a human being and she's older. And I know, through my mother, on a Thursday evening at six p.m., and my father, over the course of two very short, endless years, what happens to human beings when they get older. And this is what you decided to do with your time on Earth? And hers? I can't believe the things I thought were important on this Earth. Valuable. *(A very small, bitter laugh.)* Oh, my God.

RIGHTY. It's good we can laugh.

DONNA. You're killing your wife with sadness and grief.

RIGHTY. Yeah, but –

DONNA. – That's not one of the sentences you can say "Yeah, but" to.

RIGHTY. Just make sure we get the payment and the Cabot Pasture, and the free condemned property – again, thank you for lying directly into my wife's face – and then maybe we can have the kind of retirement Joanne talks about. You can do your project and also help some people in trouble. Look at this. *(A picture on his phone.)*

DONNA. Oh my God – high-def pictures on a smartphone. The poor old helpless invalid. *(She looks.)* Yes. I see. A boat.

RIGHTY. Look at the name.

DONNA. "The Joanne." So what. This is yours? *(Brief pause. Tries to catch him in a lie:)* What kind of boat is it? How big? Exactly.

RIGHTY. A twenty-two-foot Catalina.

DONNA. Where is it?

RIGHTY. In a warehouse in Marshwood, waiting for me to figure out a place to put it.

DONNA. When you lie all the time, you sort of stop being a person. You lose the right to open your mouth.

RIGHTY. Please just look at me. I'm sorry. I'm old and scared and poor and sorry.

He looks frail and humble and real.

DONNA. You promise to tell her everything?

RIGHTY. I do. I will. Thank you.

DONNA. If you don't, I will.

RIGHTY. Okay.

DONNA. I'm going to get us all together. You and Joanne, Tim, everyone.

RIGHTY. Just tell us where to be and when.

DONNA. And you'll sign everything?

RIGHTY. Yes. You can watch me do it.

DONNA. I will.

RIGHTY. And I won't tell her that you were defrauding us and putting us in danger. Great. Easy-peasy. *(Looks at the model and plans.)* So, this is what it's going to look like?

DONNA. Do you care?

RIGHTY. I do. It's just going to be a bunch of buildings and driveways. *(Looks around.)* This.

DONNA. *(She is staring at him.)* I thought you were so different.

RIGHTY. I was.

DONNA. So this is how you were able to arrange for the home aide person who comes by? And the meal delivery?

RIGHTY. Those things are mainly for Joanne. A little comfort and support. She's worked so hard. Please don't tell anyone.

DONNA. *(Brief pause as she ponders it all, sadly.)* Okay.

RIGHTY. I wonder if Joanne'll forgive me. I want to give her those days she dreams about.

DONNA. Maybe she just dreams about regular days, talking with you. Ordinary days with an okay husband.

RIGHTY. Maybe. I'm glad I got her the boat, just in case.

DONNA. I don't know if visible things are what she needs.

> **RIGHTY** *leaves.*
>
> **DONNA** *packs up the last few things as night falls.*
>
> *Nighttime sounds. Moonlight. The sound of a car driving away.*
>
> *Several days pass in the space of a few moments. Maybe sunrises and sunsets over the land? (Impressionistically, not in simply a speeded-up way.)*

Scene Six

Nighttime, again. Blue light of the moon. Clouds pass overhead. Some distant summer thunder and occasional lightning.

Sound and lights of a car pulling into the parking lot.

In the dark, **TIM** *enters, talking on the phone. He's carrying a flashlight, mainly aimed at the ground. He's drunk but accustomed to it.*

TIM. *(Mid-conversation:)* – Over here, at the worksite slash cemetery. There's a car in the lot, so I'm taking a look. Sort of freaking out, here, Donna. I'm on the hook for a lot more money than I've ever even seen. This is the big time. Call me when you get this, unless I'm talking to you in person right now? *(Brief pause.)* Guess it's a message. And the message is, I'm sorry. I want to make things right. *(Drinks from a pint bottle.)* Congratulations on this meeting tomorrow. Those old folks are suddenly getting in line. You did it! I knew you would, even though I said you couldn't. Things are going to move very fast after we do the signing. Once we get it all up and running, we should definitely do that Caribbean Ocean thing. *(A moment of stomach pain.)* Whoo. I got some kind of stomach issue, here. Luckily, you wear a tie to the doctors and mention pain, they give you sixty of these before you're done asking. *(Takes a pill. Quietly, pathetically:)* I'm a dumb piece of shit. I need a big change of heart. Seriously. *(A brief pause. He makes a "vrooming" truck sound:)* Vrrrrooooommmm. Vrooom. You know what that was? Trucks. Trucks zooming around. All right. Give me a call, unless I'm talking to you now, which... *(Listens for a moment.)* again, guess not. *(Walks back toward the last old grave.)* Oh, you'll never believe what I found in my car. You'll love this. I was sitting in the parking lot outside of –

For a second, the bright light of his flashlight lands on the face of a ghostly old woman, about ten feet away. **TIM** *recoils and drops his phone. She is ragged, looks like a corpse, and stands completely still. She wears a long, black dress, torn and covered with bits of dirt and moss and spiderwebs.*

TIM. You scared the shit out of me.

The figure holds up a hand to block the light. **TIM** *moves the light so she's only partially lit.*

Who is that? Are you messing with me. Just because I'm drunk, doesn't mean –

The figure makes a small movement toward **TIM**, *scaring him.*

Jesus!

He drops the flashlight, and all is dark as he tries to find it on the ground. He finally does and shines the light around the cemetery, but the figure is gone. He hurriedly stumbles off.

A glimmer of dawn. A cold sun rises, hidden by the trees.

Scene Seven

The graveyard. Bright morning sun and birdsong. **DONNA, RIGHTY,** *and* **GREY** *are sitting in and around the gazebo.* **GREY***'s finished painting is nearby: a pleasing view of the graveyard. Some food and drink sits on the gazebo table, champagne glasses, etc. In the burial area, Louise Dagenhart's headstone is gone, and the dirt around the grave is jagged and violently upturned.* **GREY** *is looking over at the mess.*

GREY. This was the guys from the funeral home?

DONNA. Yeah. Houseman's.

GREY. Wow. Kind of a smash and grab job, for a disinterment.

DONNA. It's done is all I care.

    RIGHTY *looks at* **GREY***'s painting.*

RIGHTY. This is a nice painting. What's the word?

GREY. Bucolic?

RIGHTY. Way off. Try again. It's got a vowel in it.

GREY. Bucolic has a vowel in it.

DONNA. *(To* **RIGHTY***:)* Do you get tired? Do you ever just get fucking tired?

RIGHTY. I do.

GREY. *(To* **DONNA***, with some concern:)* What's going on?

DONNA. *(Takes a breath.)* I don't know.

GREY. *(Looking at his painting. To* **RIGHTY***:)* Thanks. It does look something with a vowel in it, doesn't it. *(To* **DONNA***:)* Sonya Neubatten says I really captured the spirit.

DONNA. She's been out here?

GREY. I think she just meant in general.

DONNA. Is she the type of person – you know what, I don't care. The second we get paid, it's goodbye for me.

TIM *enters, moving a little cautiously in the previous night's rumpled clothes.*

DONNA. Whoa.

TIM. *(Very quietly:)* Morning.

He uneasily registers the torn-up grave.

What is this? Who did this?

DONNA. Houseman's. The usual guys.

GREY. I was just saying it's a pretty shoddy job. I'll be right back.

He takes his phone out and exits toward the parking lot.

DONNA. I told them ASAP, so maybe they rushed it.

RIGHTY. Morning.

He wanders off to look at a tree or plant.

DONNA. *(To* **TIM***:)* You look, wow, you look a little rough.

TIM *nods.*

Maybe you can spruce yourself up a little?

TIM. I'm all right.

DONNA. I got your message, last night.

TIM. Oh, good. What did it say?

DONNA. A few nice things, ending with a weird part. But, thank you.

TIM. Sure. Big night for me.

DONNA. Yeah?

JOANNE *enters, a little more dressed up than usual.* **RIGHTY** *joins her.*

JOANNE. *(To* **TIM***:)* There are no paper towels in there.

TIM. Good morning. I don't care about that.

DONNA. Morning, Joanne.

GREY *enters.*

JOANNE. Hello. *(Sits.)* Tell me why we're signing all this again.

DONNA. Everything just has to be exactly right, without edits or anything being crossed out. And Righty made a few small –

JOANNE. – You're sure we shouldn't have a lawyer here?

DONNA. You can if you like, but it's all very simple.

JOANNE. *(Looking at the contracts:)* It doesn't look very simple.

DONNA. *(As she's spreading out the three contracts:)* This is the agreement that covers the plot here, and the payment terms. The deed for the Cabot Pasture. *(To* **RIGHTY***:)* Your special place. *(To* **RIGHTY** *and* **JOANNE***:)* And this is the paperwork on the house.

JOANNE. So, the same things as before.

DONNA. Yes. All pretty standard, but very exciting.

She hands **JOANNE** *and* **RIGHTY** *each a pen.*

RIGHTY. Can we keep these?

JOANNE. I'm sure you can keep the pen.

RIGHTY. *(Looks at it.)* Not as nice as U-Haul.

JOANNE. He got an orange pen from U-Haul that he likes. And these are my golden years.

RIGHTY. What?

JOANNE. You like your U-Haul pen.

DONNA. Does he like his U-Haul penny wenny?

RIGHTY. He does. It's got a good click. I hope a house doesn't fall down on my head while I'm using it.

DONNA. What a mess that would be for your fully-funded-by-the-state twenty-hour-a-week home healthcare worker.

JOANNE. I don't think any roof is going to fall in. *(To* **RIGHTY***:)* We could stop by the U-Haul place and I bet they'd give you another one.

TIM. *(To* **JOANNE** *and* **RIGHTY***:)* You two have something very beautiful and rare.

JOANNE. Thank you.

DONNA *restrains herself from showing her exasperation.*

JOANNE. *(As she's signing:)* What we have is a quiet one-way street most of the time, but, thank you.

RIGHTY. We have a lot of fun. It's a very successful marriage.

JOANNE. *(Warmly:)* Oh is it?

She moves on to the next contract and prepares to sign. **TIM** *looks at it.*

TIM. Is that one for the Cabot land? For the pasture?

DONNA. Yeah. *(To* **JOANNA***:)* Your special present to your husband.

TIM *takes those contracts.*

TIM. Let's hold off on this one, okay?

JOANNE. I'm sorry? No. I'm here to sign that.

DONNA. This was one of the first things we discussed.

TIM. I'm probably not thinking clearly today, but, this is what I'm thinking. So I'll just tear these in half. Like so. *(He does it.)* Voila.

DONNA. What are you doing?

RIGHTY. What was that?

JOANNE. Your pasture, in the blackberries. Since they're digging up the cemetery.

TIM. I'm good with everything else. Sign those and we're all set.

RIGHTY. Let's go get some grilled cheese sandwiches.

JOANNE. Righty, please – I'm right in the middle of something. *(To* **TIM***:)* I don't think I understand.

TIM. You think you can scare me?

JOANNE. No.

DONNA. *(To* **RIGHTY** *and* **JOANNE***:)* I'm sorry about this. I have another copy in my car.

JOANNE. I made a promise to my husband – don't listen, dear – which I broke. I broke it in exchange for this little patch of the world where he could go, and feel okay, someplace that wouldn't get ruined. And now you're telling us No?

TIM. I'm telling you no.

JOANNE. I see.

RIGHTY. *(To* **TIM***:)* We don't have any place that's ours. We don't have any place to go. We don't have any money.

TIM. You will if you sign a couple pieces of paper. But no Cabot Pasture.

DONNA. It's just an empty pasture. So now that's getting developed with the rest of it?

JOANNE. You know what? I think grilled cheeses is a great idea. Let's go, Righty.

She starts to get up.

TIM. Let's not get greedy. *(Referring to paperwork:)* Here's the paperwork on the house right here, and I'll transfer my very generous payment to you right now.

RIGHTY. Maybe there's some kind of a rider you could attach to the agreement that provides for a – what was I just sayin–

DONNA. – Would you please just shut the fuck up?!

RIGHTY. Okay.

TIM. *(To* **JOANNE** *and* **RIGHTY***:)* Interesting approach.

JOANNE. Why are you treating us like this? Is this a…is this some scheme to trick us?

TIM. She's been working very hard.

GREY. I'd take it. Whatever they're offering. Such uncertain times, you know?

JOANNE. You think we should do this?

DONNA. *(To* **GREY***:)* What?

GREY. Sometimes, I don't know, you just have to face things realistically.

TIM. Well said. Well said.

DONNA. *(To* **JOANNE***:)* It *is* quite a lot. I just believe when people promise to do things, they should do them.

RIGHTY. Maybe they will.

JOANNE. *(To* **DONNA***:)* What promise are you talking about?

TIM. *(To* **JOANNE***:)* You have a very good deal here.

JOANNE. *(To* **GREY***:)* You think we should go ahead with this?

GREY. It's not my place but I do.

JOANNE. I guess sometimes things change and we have to try to be understanding.

TIM. Yes, we do.

JOANNE. *(Sadly, to* **RIGHTY***:)* We'll find you another place, okay? With moss and blackberries and all of it. I promise.

RIGHTY. I wanted it to be forever, but okay.

> **JOANNE** *looks at* **RIGHTY**. *She begins to sign the documents.*
>
> **DONNA** *quietly points.*

DONNA. Where the little sticker – yes. And initial here.

> **JOANNE** *initials the document.*

TIM. *(To* **GREY***:)* I'm glad you saw the light.

GREY. It wasn't really light I saw.

TIM. Well, whatever.

RIGHTY. Do I sign too?

JOANNE. Yes. *(To* **DONNA***:)* Yes?

DONNA. Yeah, there and there. And he needs to initial.

> **RIGHTY** *signs and initials.* **TIM** *checks the documents. Hands one back to* **JOANNE**, *pointing:*

TIM. Date.

JOANNE. *(Checks her phone for the date.)* I won't soon forget this day. *(Writes the date.)*

> **TIM** *checks again and begins to make a transaction on his phone.*

DONNA. The house is really very sweet.

RIGHTY. And it's ours?

DONNA. You don't have to do a thing.

TIM. *(Finishing transaction on his phone:)* "Transfer complete." Congratulations. It's in your account.

JOANNE. You won't be insulted if I make sure?

TIM. Just a little. No, go ahead.

> **JOANNE** *reads a phone number from a business card and dials.*

JOANNE. Excuse me. *(Steps away. To phone:)* Hello, this is Joanne Morse. May I speak with Robin Jacoby... *(Inaudible.)*

TIM. *(To* **RIGHTY***:)* Hi. *(Very brief pause.)* You think I sent it?

RIGHTY. You said you did.

GREY. Now you're going to torture the poor man?

TIM. I figure that land must have some other qualities.

DONNA. Okay, but, still, so you just rip up the whole –

> **JOANNE** *returns.*

JOANNE. It's all there, in full. *(To* **TIM***:)* Thank you.

TIM. Sure. Congratulations. That's a serious pile of money.

JOANNE. I wasn't sure it would be there, to be honest.

DONNA. I can understand that. How do you feel?

JOANNE. I feel a few different things.

DONNA. I hope one of them is, just, you know, security.

JOANNE. That isn't one of them, no. *(Picks up the folders and paperwork.)* Okay, Righty, let's go.

DONNA. This probably sounds crazy, but, now that we're through all this stuff, I predict a difficult but really beautiful change in your life.

JOANNE. Do you.

DONNA. I know, that's a very personal thing to say, and you know, who am I?

JOANNE. Yes. Who are you.

RIGHTY. What's she saying?

JOANNE. I don't know. *(To* **DONNA***:)* Thank you for your prediction.

DONNA. *(To* **RIGHTY***:)* What do you think about my prediction of a difficult but beautiful change in your wife's life?

RIGHTY. Yup. Could be. I think it's a good prediction.

JOANNE. Is that champagne?

TIM. It is.

He sips some and checks his phone.

JOANNE. Oh. How civilized. Come on, Richard.

TIM. Have a good day.

RIGHTY. *(As they're moving off:)* What are they celebrating?

JOANNE. You'd have to ask them.

DONNA. *(Waves.)* Bye. Congrats, again.

TIM. You forgot your pen.

JOANNE. Could we speak with someone about Righty's headstone?

DONNA. Oh, um...

TIM *points at* **GREY**.

GREY. Please call whenever you like. My card is in there.

JOANNE *and* **RIGHTY** *exit.*

DONNA. What was that? Why did you do that?

TIM. To make money.

DONNA. It's a meaningless mess of brambles.

GREY. I don't think land can be meaningless.

TIM. That land is going to skyrocket. That's why I was happy to pay top dollar.

DONNA. But you had to do it like that?

TIM. *(Looking toward former site of Dagenhart grave:)* I had some realizations recently.

DONNA. Was one that you need to lie and go back on your word?

TIM. Life's short.

DONNA. *(Frustrated and confused with this response:)* I'm not going to let you ruin this.

TIM. Good thinking.

DONNA. I thought this would feel different, more like working on the Armory. But that's all right.

TIM. This is a triumph, no question. A lot of moments like this are kind of empty inside. You have to sort of thrive on that feeling.

> *In the following exchange there is frustration and also mutual recognition of the excitement of getting things done:*

DONNA. Goddamnit, Tim.

TIM. Goddamnit, Donna.

DONNA. They'll be okay, right?

TIM. They'll be better than that. And we're going to be amazing. Goddamnit, us.

> *The sun gets bright. Some natural afternoon sounds.*

It's funny, when I went to buy that pasture it turned out one of the Cabot kids had just sold it to some little real estate group, two days before. But the new owner was very happy to sell it right off to me, making themselves a pretty astronomical profit. I paid a pretty hefty price. But still nowhere near what it's worth.

DONNA. It was someone local?

TIM. I'd never heard of them. I just dealt with the lawyer.

> *He looks at his watch.*

DONNA. When's Neubatten getting here?

TIM. Half hour.

DONNA. That's cutting it close.

TIM. That's how things work.

DONNA. Then what?

TIM. We cross the I's and dot the T's with Neubatten, and then we get paid. Half up front, and half when the first shovel gets picked up. He was grousing about our back-end percentages last week, but even if it got cut in half, which it won't, we still make out like bandits.

DONNA. But we're not bandits.

TIM. No. Then I want to pitch you an interesting little idea. And I'm going to drink this champagne before it gets warm.

GREY. Can I have some of that?

TIM. Sure.

DONNA. You're celebrating?

GREY. Just thirsty.

He holds up a glass.

TIM. *(Pouring:)* There you are, sir. Someone really put a scare into me, last night.

GREY. Oh yeah?

TIM. Yeah.

*He looks at **GREY** for a while. Then at **DONNA**.*

Real bad scare. Champagne?

DONNA. *(Getting a glass. Small laugh.)* Are we ridiculous, drinking champagne in the morning?

TIM. No. I realized, last night, if someone's going to try so hard to scare me off this thing, then I must be on the right track. The last piece was the Cabot dealie.

He looks over at the grave area.

When we're done with Neubatten, let's you and me go somewhere quiet where we can –

His phone rings. He checks to see who's calling.

Boom. Here we go. *(Answers.)* Paul, hello! *(Brief pauses where necessary:)* Oh, hi, Teddy – I saw his name come up. What's that? And I appreciate *his* time. But, so what are you actually –? Well, I assume a "low feasibility score" means that he's – yes, okay. But a lot of money's been spent here based on an agreement I made with –. Well, a verbal agreement is still a – *(Listens for a long time.)* Can I speak with him – I'd like to speak with him. I don't want to have to get my lawyer involv–. Okay, well, please do that, thank –. *(Puts his phone away.)* You fucking little...

DONNA. What? Oh, Jesus, no. What'd they say?

> TIM *nods, and then keeps nodding some more, looking pretty desperate. He doesn't have words. He refills his glass with champagne and leaves.*

What's going on? Tim, what is happening?

TIM. *(Quietly, to no one, as he's exiting:)* A salamander.

DONNA. What? Can you call someone over at Neubatten's office?

GREY. I could try.

DONNA. I gave up all the things I gave up for this? For nothing?! *(Brief pause.)* Did he say "salamander"?

GREY. I think so.

DONNA. I cannot...is this just all over? After everything I did. *(Very brief pause.)* You don't look surprised.

GREY. No, I'm surprised. But maybe I've looked surprised the entire time you've known me, so you don't really have a baseline.

> *Lights. Natural events and sounds.*

Scene Eight

The graveyard. A couple weeks later. Dusk. Things have been partly tended to, holes filled, etc. A shovel and large pry bar sit in a wheelbarrow, which sits near Righty's gravesite. **JOANNE** *is sitting nearby on a collapsible portable camp stool. She contemplates the gravesite and the surrounding area.*

Some clouds pass over the cemetery, a mysterious shadow or odd moment that **JOANNE** *notices.*

GREY *enters with some cardboard and tape.*

GREY. I knew I brought this stuff.

He wraps the still-standing gravestone with cardboard, talking while he works.

JOANNE. Thank you, again.

GREY. No, of course. Especially after everything with Righty.

JOANNE. Oh, how that man has aged me. *(Very brief pause.)* I guess I would've gotten just as old, just as quick, without him.

GREY. *(Small, warm smile.)* I guess.

He begins to work the gravestone loose with the pry bar.

JOANNE. We'll come out here soon. Just to sit. When we recover from...from all this.

GREY. That was rough how things worked out.

JOANNE. But you know what, that land probably would've just turned into another burden. Can you believe it, Righty had taken out a loan, just for his place here, and to try to make up for the deposit we lost at the other cemetery.

GREY. So maybe you got lucky.

JOANNE. So what's going to happen here?

GREY. Things really took a turn when they discovered the salamander breeding pools near here. That species turned out to be federally protected, so that allowed the Neubattens to be involved in a whole different way.

The gravestone moves a little bit.

Here we go.

He rocks it back and forth until it's free.

JOANNE. *(A sad but loving little laugh.)* Oh, Righty – you and your plans. Do you know he once tried to buy a boat trailer? *(As she watches the gravestone being pried out of the ground:)* I don't think a lot of spouses get to see this particular scene. It feels like the fall of a foreign country – you know, when they pull down the statues.

GREY. How're you doing with it all?

JOANNE. Oh, I don't know. The whole thing, the reality underneath all this, is so strange – a person in a box in the ground. Night and day, rain or shine – dead, dead, dead. Cemeteries send out color brochures, as if it's like anything else.

The gravestone is free. **GREY** *lifts it out.*

And, I guess that's that.

Brief pause. **JOANNE** *looks around, quietly, not knowing where to look.*

Finito.

GREY *finds something in the dirt.*

What'd you find?

GREY. A piece of clay. Little shard of a bowl, maybe?

He hands it to **JOANNE.**

JOANNE. You have good eyes. Someone had a meal, a thousand years ago.

She hands it back. **GREY** *begins to lift out the gravestone.*

Can you get it?

GREY. I think so.

> *He lifts it and puts it into the wheelbarrow.*
> *There are no gravestones left.*

JOANNE. Now it's just a little area.

GREY. Did you know there's fourteen dead people for every living person on Earth? I sometimes like to think of them being here, but not here, but here. Like there's some wisdom or feeling that just kind of flows around. *(Brief pause.)* Is your car open?

JOANNE. Yes. Thank you, Grey.

> **GREY** *wheels the gravestone off.* **JOANNE** *looks around. She sits down where* **RIGHTY** *would've been buried. She drifts off somewhere. She speaks from a strange, but very calm and real place in herself.*
>
> *Some distant thunder. Dark clouds.*

I'm holding on to someone big and falling asleep. I'm climbing a tree. Tommy Honeybell and I are making a race car. I'm by my mother's bed, in the afternoon. I'm at my desk, answering the phone. I'm on a date, trying snails for the first time. I'm nervous and my father's saying, "You look beautiful. Righty is a good man." I'm reading the directions for a new crockpot. I'm putting one hundred little Post-it Notes in the recycling. I'm here. Five hundred years go by. I'm here. Does anybody know?

> *Lights fade, and then dawn approaches. Morning, evening, night, clouds, stars, and so on.*

Scene Nine

The graveyard. Morning. Weeks later. In the distance, a small marching band is heard warming up, occasional musical flourishes, a crowd, and perhaps muffled sounds of a microphone check, etc.

DONNA *enters in a casual business outfit, carrying balloons tied to small signs (arrows on sticks, to mark a walking path). She places a sign.*

TIM *is hidden somewhere, maybe behind the gazebo, drinking from a fast-food cup.*

TIM. Fancy meeting you here.

DONNA. *(Startled:)* Jesus!

TIM. Did you get a job putting little signs and balloons around in the woods?

DONNA. It would appear.

TIM. Maybe you made a bad decision.

DONNA. Maybe.

TIM. What's the, what's going on here?

DONNA. A lot.

TIM. You look nice.

DONNA. Thank you.

TIM. *(Sadly:)* You fucking stole the whole deal, behind my back. Everything I did.

DONNA. I would never do that. Actually, I might, but I didn't, in this case.

TIM. You're Neubatten's inside person, now?

DONNA. I'm working on the future Sonya & Paul Neubatten Natural Wildlife Refuge. In which you're standing.

TIM. Ah. That sounds like a not-for-the-slightest-bit-of-profit organization.

DONNA. It is. But, you know, there's something I get with this job that I never got with you.

TIM. Self-respect?

DONNA. Oh wow, two things – I was going to say Comprehensive Dental.

TIM. I saw something was happening here. I thought the town was taking it over. Why haven't you called me back?

DONNA. I've been busy. Also, I didn't want to.

TIM. I can understand that. But, hey, Donna? I've changed.

DONNA. Well, good. We should all be given the chance to be our best selves.

TIM. No, I mean, I've gotten worse, much worse. No question. Very dark days.

DONNA. Oh. And?

TIM. There's not always an "and."

DONNA. What do you want me to say?

TIM. A few things. That you miss me. I want you to say that you screwed me over. I know that old couple was up to something – him especially, and you can help me prove it. I think maybe the St. Onge Trust, that I bought the Cabot land from, got some inside information from him or something. And I want you to say that you'll help me recover my expenses from Neubatten. And, that you noticed I'm wearing workout stuff. And that you'll have a drink with me later.

DONNA. I *did* notice the workout clothes.

TIM. Squats are my main thing. I don't know why, I just really relate.

DONNA. *Who* did you buy the Cabot land from?

TIM. The St. Onge Trust. It's an LLC, I can't find out anything about them. Why?

DONNA. No reason. It's a memorable name.

She puts her arms around **TIM**'s *neck.*

Ooh, so clammy. I do sort of miss you. Your raw negative energy.

TIM. I thought so.

DONNA. I think the Morses are just trying to survive old age, any way they can.

TIM. You think they're victims. They're not victims.

DONNA. And I stopped drinking – so, no thanks, on the drinks invitation. Things are marginally better – but that's good. I think marginally is good. Okay, I should get back to my little signs and balloons.

She separates from him.

TIM. That's it? And so now what do you want *me* to say?

DONNA. I really don't care, Tim. "Good job"? "Nice touch with the open-air classroom near the babbling brook"?

GREY *enters with cushions for the gazebo seats. He's dressed in a suit.*

GREY. Hi.

TIM *looks at him and doesn't respond.*

How's it going here? Everything okay?

DONNA. I think we're in good shape.

TIM. Everyone's involved in this thing, huh?

GREY. Well, not everyone. I mean, you're not.

TIM. I thought you had some ambition. You're working on this pile of leaves and worms?

GREY. I'm the Executive Director of this pile of leaves and worms.

TIM. I'm glad I got my piece of the pie with the Cabot land, though.

GREY. He doesn't know?

TIM. What? What I know is, I've got two acres of primo real estate, abutting a nature reserve.

GREY. You're the man.

DONNA. Neubatten bought all the acreage around that parcel, in exchange for a pretty hefty tax abatement. And now it's all been declared protected lands, in perpetuity.

TIM. *(Brief pause.)* You don't think someone's going to want to build a McMansion with a view of all that?

DONNA. Except that there can't be any access roads. So nobody can get to the two acres. No electricity or water, or anything.

TIM. I'll put in a fucking helicopter pad.

DONNA. Ooh, good idea.

GREY. There might be regulations about noise.

TIM. Were you two plotting behind my back the whole time?

DONNA.	**GREY.**
It's funny, we were not, no.	This came together totally organically.

TIM. *(To* **GREY***:)* I thought it was "a balance," between nature and development.

GREY. I did too. But it turns out it isn't. There's the Earth, on which we live, and that's pretty much it.

TIM. And so now you two are the great saviors? Giving the goddess Earth what she wants?

DONNA. Yes.

GREY. It's funny, nature probably doesn't care if this is a graveyard, or animal refuge, or shopping mall. Nature'll do what it does, one way or another.

TIM. What are you, starting a cult?

GREY. Actually, we're structured as a limited liability corporation. Sustainable landscape architecture and wetlands protection. Donna's going to run that, since I've got this place.

TIM. Sounds like you've got a real vision.

DONNA. There's a difference between garbage piled up in a parking lot, and wildflowers and tall grasses, gently blowing in the wind. There's a difference. And the difference is either important to you, or it isn't.

TIM. *(To* **DONNA***:)* I never lied to you.

DONNA. Really? And? Oh, just remembered, there's not always an and.

TIM. I guess you're feeling very superior.

DONNA. A little.

TIM. That's only because the person you think you want to be is slightly better than the person I actually authentically am.

DONNA. That might be true. I will certainly give it some thought.

GREY. We probably all do some version of that, a little.

TIM. I'm going to haunt you. I will haunt you.

DONNA. Okay. *(Very brief pause.)* It's funny, I've always felt haunted, sort of, like it was my fate. But now I'm trying to only be haunted by real things. The truth, things I wish I'd told my mom and dad, skinny polar bears swimming in circles until they sink, time, rivers clogged with dead frogs, real things like that. But not you. Not some living former co-worker.

GREY. I like that. "Good things to be haunted by."

DONNA. Thanks.

> **GREY** *busies himself off to the side.*

TIM. You can't do this to me.

DONNA. Oh, okay.

TIM. I will be back, in every single way.

DONNA. I'm sure you will be. See you then.

> **JOANNE** *enters as* **TIM** *is leaving. She is walking with a cane and wearing protective UV-blocking sunglasses of the kind people wear after cataract surgery.* **TIM** *stands before her.*

JOANNE. *(To* **TIM***:)* Is that Grey? I just had eye surgery.

> **TIM** *goes past without speaking.*

GREY. Hi, Joanne. Here I am. You look like you've been through the wringer. Did you get a look at the guy who did this to you?

JOANNE. I did. He was wearing a white coat and a stethoscope.

GREY. The monster. What happened to your leg?

JOANNE. I broke a bone in my foot. The stairs – that little house of ours needs some work.

DONNA. Oh no. Well, we're so glad you're here. Come sit down. How's Righty doing?

JOANNE. Oh, that man.

DONNA. I was hoping he might join us for the ribbon-cutting.

JOANNE. We all have hopes.

DONNA. Oh, guess what?

> **JOANNE** *sits on the new park bench, in her dark glasses, resting her hands on her cane, staring out.*

GREY. Maybe she doesn't feel like playing a guessing game.

DONNA. We named one of the walking trails after Righty.

> *Sound of a text message arriving in* **GREY***'s phone.*

GREY. *(Checks his phone.)* Teddy's here. *(Reading text:)* He says, "No Paul today, but I have a statement from him."

DONNA. Has anyone ever actually seen that man?

GREY. *(Sending a text as he exits:)* I'll meet you over there?

DONNA. Yeah. *(To* **JOANNE***:)* So…how are you both?

JOANNE. *(Looking to where Righty's grave was:)* How would you be? One minute you think everything is some particular way, and the next…

DONNA. It must've been a real shock. I don't think I could've managed.

JOANNE. Well, I'm sure you'll find the strength, when you need it.

DONNA. Well, I hope – sorry, but I hope I never have to face something like that.

JOANNE. Someone getting older?

DONNA. No. Did Righty tell you?

JOANNE. Tell me what? My husband tells me everything. He can't help it.

DONNA. I think he can.

JOANNE. It's dangerous to think you know everything about other people. It also must be exhausting. Is your life perfect?

DONNA. No.

JOANNE. Is it even close?

DONNA. No.

JOANNE. Nor is mine. But we're settling into our home, as creaky as it may be. I planted some tomatoes and onions. It feels good to get your fingernails dirty.

> **RIGHTY** *enters, quietly, taking cautious and small steps.* **JOANNE** *hasn't seen him, because of her eyes and dark glasses, and he's out of* **DONNA**'s *sightline. He's quietly arrived behind her.*

DONNA. I'm sorry if I seemed –

She's startled by **RIGHTY**.

What is it with people just appearing and disappearing around here.

JOANNE. *(Turning:)* Is that – who's there?

DONNA. Your husband.

JOANNE. How did you get over here?

RIGHTY. *(His speech is a little unclear, and quiet:)* Melanie.

JOANNE. Oh, Melanie. You like her. *(To* **DONNA**:*)* It's this great organization where people come over to read him books.

DONNA. What a nice idea. How're you doing, Righty?

> **RIGHTY** *shrugs.*

RIGHTY. Life.

JOANNE. They say the old him could be coming back any day. So we do our practice, vocabulary and what things are. Don't we.

RIGHTY. Mm-hmm.

DONNA. Well…keep at it. *(To* **RIGHTY**:*)* You look very well.

A brief pause as she waits for a response.

JOANNE. We used to share so much. And now here we are.

DONNA. *(To* **RIGHTY***:)* Did you have a chance, did you guys talk, before Righty's – what was it?

JOANNE. A stroke. A small stroke.

DONNA. But before that happened, Righty, did you tell her?

JOANNE. Tell me what? *(To* **RIGHTY***, with warmth and lightness:)* You did say you had some big news.

> *A brief pause in which* **RIGHTY** *has a tiny response, as if some small, lost part of him wants to respond.*

(To **DONNA***, again, lightly:)* He was always planning something.

> **RIGHTY** *looks up in the air, like he's reading skywriting.*

Welcome to my life.

DONNA. But it's not. This isn't your life. This isn't real.

JOANNE. No, I think this is probably very real.

DONNA. Righty, you can't do this. Would you say something?! Please say something now!

> **RIGHTY** *looks at her. He smiles, with a pained expression of wanting to understand. He looks to* **JOANNE**.

JOANNE. *(To* **DONNA***:)* Getting mad doesn't help.

DONNA. You don't understand.

JOANNE. I know what you're trying to do.

DONNA. I don't think you do.

> **TIM** *enters. Followed by* **GREY***, who protectively keeps an eye on him.*

Tim, this really isn't the time.

GREY. Or the place.

TIM. This was my thing. I want to speak to Paul.

GREY. He's not here.

DONNA. Why don't you head home.

GREY. We can call you a cab, if you need one.

JOANNE. *(To* **DONNA**, *quietly:)* That's Mr. Tyson?

DONNA. It is.

JOANNE. Hello.

TIM. I know what you're doing.

JOANNE. I'm glad someone does. Let us ladies finish talking please.

>   **TIM** *goes over to the gazebo, to sit.*

DONNA. Yes, we really do need to talk.

JOANNE. Donna, I appreciate you yelling at my diminished husband.

DONNA. No, of course. No, I mean, he's not diminished.

JOANNE. It's completely understandable to get angry. But these are the facts. The wonderful, impossible facts. *(A tiny little gesture.)* Here's this little area, here, and here we all are, trying to find room for ourselves, trying to find our place in it.

DONNA. *(Takes in her beautiful surroundings. Quietly:)* Does anybody find it? A place for themselves? At least the feeling of it?

GREY. I think so. I think people do.

JOANNE. We all have a final resting place, like it or not. It's probably never going to be the one we've imagined.

TIM. I have a lot of thoughts. I've got a lot of thoughts here.

RIGHTY. Wah-wah.

>   **JOANNE** *gives him a water bottle with a straw in it and he takes a sip.*

JOANNE. He can say water, but he couldn't for a while, so we still joke. Wah-wah.

>   *Some more stray sounds of a band warming up, some excited crowd noise, coming from over in the parking lot area.*

GREY. *(Checking his watch, to* **DONNA**:*)* We should start heading over. *(While checking his phone:)* You okay?

DONNA. *(Surprisingly moved:)* You really mean that, don't you.

GREY. *(A tiny little laugh.)* What? It's just a normal little question, but, yeah. I mean it.

DONNA. Thanks. *(Very brief pause. Sadly, or at least, complicatedly:)* This is a very happy day.

GREY. It is.

RIGHTY. *(Very quietly:)* The rain in France...in Spain... *(Very brief pause.)* A, E, I, O, U. *(Looks around.)* U. U.

DONNA. Are you saying that to me?

>   **RIGHTY** *doesn't respond.*

JOANNE. He was always a people person. Righty, should we do some practice?

RIGHTY. Okay.

>   **DONNA** *and* **GREY** *move off, but turn to watch* **JOANNE** *and* **RIGHTY.**
>
>   **TIM** *remains, over in the gazebo.*

JOANNE. Where are we?

RIGHTY. Outdoors.

JOANNE. Yes. It's going to stay like this, mossy and green. But no more burying people. They said there's something with your name on it here, a trail. *(Looking off:)* And what's that?

RIGHTY. A house.

JOANNE. Yes, it's a gazebo. Remember that one? *(Very brief pause.)* It's a tricky one.

RIGHTY. Yeah. Now you.

JOANNE. Okay. *(To **DONNA** and others:)* He likes me to practice too. What should I say?

RIGHTY. Pretend I'm lost.

JOANNE. Okay. *(A little amused. To **DONNA** and others:)* Aren't we mysterious creatures? Where does it all come from?

RIGHTY. Say...pretend you say..."Righty? Oh, Richard? Where are you?"

JOANNE. Righty? Oh, Richard? Where are you?
RIGHTY. *(He looks out.)* Good.
Lights fade.

End of Play

www.ingramcontent.com/pod-product-compliance
Lightning Source LLC
Chambersburg PA
CBHW072018290426
44109CB00018B/2278